to:

from:

date:

teen
SERIES
devos

WHO AM I?

100 Days of Discovery

FAMILY CHRISTIAN STORES
Grand Rapids, MI 49530

The quoted ideas expressed in this book (but not scripture verses) are not, in all cases, exact quotations, as some have been edited for clarity and brevity. In all cases, the author has attempted to maintain the speaker's original intent. In some cases, quoted material for this book was obtained from secondary sources, primarily print media. While every effort was made to ensure the accuracy of these sources, the accuracy cannot be guaranteed. For additions, deletions, corrections or clarifications in future editions of this text, please write FAMILY CHRISTIAN STORES.

Scripture quotations are taken from:

The Holy Bible, King James Version

The Holy Bible, New International Version (NIV) Copyright © 1973, 1978, 1984, by International Bible Society. Used by permission of Zondervan Publishing House. All rights reserved.

The New American Standard Bible®, (NASB) Copyright © 1960, 1962, 1963, 1968, 1971, 1972, 1973, 1975, 1977, 1995 by The Lockman Foundation. Used by permission.

The Holy Bible, New King James Version (NKJV) Copyright © 1982 by Thomas Nelson, Inc. Used by permission.

The Holy Bible, New Living Translation, (NLT) Copyright © 1996. Used by permission of Tyndale House Publishers, Inc., Wheaton, Illinois 60189. All rights reserved.

New Century Version®. (NCV) Copyright © 1987, 1988, 1991 by Word Publishing, a division of Thomas Nelson, Inc. All rights reserved. Used by permission.

The Message (MSG) This edition issued by contractual arrangement with NavPress, a division of The Navigators, U.S.A. Originally published by NavPress in English as THE MESSAGE: The Bible in Contemporary Language copyright 2002-2003 by Eugene Peterson. All rights reserved.

The Holman Christian Standard Bible™ (HCSB) Copyright © 1999, 2000, 2001 by Holman Bible Publishers. Used by permission.

Cover Design by Kim Russell / Wahoo Designs
Page Layout by Bart Dawson

ISBN 978-1-60587-062-5

Printed in the United States of America

teen
SERIES
devos

WHO AM I?
100 Days of Discovery

Introduction

Who am I? It's a question that you may find easier to ask than to answer. If so, this book can help you sort things out.

As you know from firsthand experience, it isn't easy being a young person in our 21st-century world. Every day, you are confronted with countless opportunities to wander far from the path that God intends for you to take. Every day, you come face-to-face with questions, temptations, and distractions that were unknown to previous generations. Every day, you have difficult choices to make—choices that can help you become the person God wants you be . . . or not. And make no mistake: the results of your choices will have far reaching consequences.

This book contains 100 brief devotional readings that are intended to help you figure out who you are today and who you want to become tomorrow. Are you facing difficult decisions? Are you seeking to change some aspect of your life? Do you want to gain a better understanding of the person you are and the person you can be in the future? If so, ask for God's help and ask for it many times each day . . . starting with a regular, heartfelt morning devotional. When you do, you will change your day . . . and your life.

Who Are You?
You Are a Person Who Puts God First

Jesus answered, "'Love the Lord your God with all your heart,
all your soul, and all your mind.'
This is the first and most important command."
Matthew 22:37-38 NCV

If you want to figure out who you are—and who you want to become—you should be aware that self-understanding, like every other good thing in this universe, starts with God. In other words, you can't have a healthy relationship with yourself until you have a healthy relationship with your Creator.

As you think about the nature of your relationship with God, remember this: you will always have some type of relationship with Him—it is inevitable that your life must be lived in relationship to God. The question is not if you will have a relationship with Him; the burning question is whether or not that relationship will be one that seeks to honor Him.

Are you willing to place God first in your life? And, are you willing to welcome God's Son into your heart? Unless you can honestly answer these questions with a resounding yes, then your relationship with God isn't what it could be or should be. Thankfully, God is always available, He's always ready to forgive, and He's waiting to hear from you now. The rest, of course, is up to you.

Jesus challenges you and me to keep our focus daily on the cross of His will if we want to be His disciples.

Anne Graham Lotz

Whatever you love most, be it sports, pleasure, business or God, that is your god.

Billy Graham

You must never sacrifice your relationship with God for the sake of a relationship with another person.

Charles Stanley

Today, spend a few minutes thinking about your relationship with God. Is it really an intimate one-on-one connection, or are you allowing other things to come between you and your Creator? Write down three specific steps that you can take right now to forge a stronger bond with your Heavenly Father.

Who Are You?
You Are a Person Who Doesn't Settle
for Second, Third, or Fourth Best

But as for you, be strong; don't be discouraged,
for your work has a reward.
2 Chronicles 15:7 HCSB

Do you believe that you deserve the best, and that you can achieve the best? Or have you convinced yourself that you're a second-tier talent who'll be lucky to finish far back in the pack? Before you answer that question, remember this: God sent His Son so that you might enjoy the abundant life that Jesus describes in the familiar words of John 10:10. But, God's gifts are not guaranteed—it's up to you to claim them.

As you plan for the next stage of your life's journey, promise yourself that when it comes to the important things in life, you won't settle for second best. And what, pray tell, are the "important things"? Your faith, your family, your health, and your relationships, for starters. In each of these areas, you deserve to be a rip-roaring, top-drawer success.

So if you want to achieve the best that life has to offer, convince yourself that you have the ability to earn the rewards you desire. Become sold on yourself—sold on your opportunities, sold on your potential, sold on your abilities. If you're sold on yourself, chances are the world will soon become sold, too, and the results will be beautiful.

If, in your working hours, you make the work your end,
you will presently find yourself all unawares inside
the only circle in your profession that really matters.
You will be one of the sound craftsmen,
and other sound craftsmen will know it.

C. S. Lewis

Few things fire up a person's commitment
like dedication to excellence.

John Maxwell

We are always making an offering.
If we do not give to God, we give to the devil.

Vance Havner

Don't "settle" for less: too many people find it is easy to "settle" for second-best, third-best, one millionth-best, or somewhere in between. Don't make that mistake. Ask God for the courage, the perseverance, and the wisdom to select the "first-best" path for you, and don't settle for anything less.

Who Are You?
You Are a Person Who Understands That God Loves You (and You Should, Too)

The unfailing love of the Lord never ends!
Lamentations 3:22 NLT

Face it: sometimes it can be tough to respect yourself—and tough to figure out exactly who you are—if you're feeling like a less-than-perfect citizen living in a world that seems to demand perfection. But before you go headlong into the self-criticism mode, think about this: God knows all your imperfections, all your faults, and all your shortcomings . . . and He loves you anyway. And because God loves you, you can—and should—feel good about the person you see when you look into the mirror.

If you've ever had the feeling that you simply don't "measure up," perhaps you've been measuring yourself by society's standards, not God's. If so, it's time to start worrying less about impressing other people and more about pleasing God. Starting now.

I am convinced our hearts are not healthy until
they have been satisfied by the only completely healthy love
that exists: the love of God Himself.

Beth Moore

God loves you and wants you to experience peace and life—
abundant and eternal.

Billy Graham

Being loved by Him whose opinion matters most gives us
the security to risk loving, too—even loving ourselves.

Gloria Gaither

The hope we have in Jesus is the anchor for the soul—
something sure and steadfast, preventing drifting
or giving way, lowered to the depth of God's love.

Franklin Graham

God's love makes everything look a lot better: When you invite
the love of God into your heart, everything in the world looks
different, including you.

Who Are You?
You Are a Person Who Understands
That Faith Can Move Mountains

I assure you: If anyone says to this mountain,
"Be lifted up and thrown into the sea," and does not doubt
in his heart, but believes that what he says will happen,
it will be done for him.
Mark 11:23 HCSB

Because we live in a demanding world, all of us have mountains to climb and mountains to move. Moving those mountains requires faith.

Every life—including yours—is a series of wins and losses. Every step of the way, through every triumph and tragedy, God walks with you, ready and willing to strengthen you. So the next time you find your courage tested to the limit, remember to take your fears to God. If you call upon Him, you will be comforted. Whatever your challenge, whatever your trouble, God can handle it.

When you place your faith, your trust, indeed your life in the hands of your Heavenly Father, you'll be amazed at the marvelous things He can do with you and through you. So strengthen your faith through praise, through worship, through Bible study, and through prayer. And trust God's plans. With Him, all things are possible, and He stands ready to open a world of possibilities to you . . . if you have faith.

And now, with no more delays, let the mountain moving begin.

I do not want merely to possess a faith;
I want a faith that possesses me.

Charles Kingsley

The essence of the Christian life is Jesus: that in all things He might have the preeminence,
not that in some things He might have a place.

Franklin Graham

The heaviest end of the cross lies ever on His shoulders.
If He bids us carry a burden, He carries it also.

C. H. Spurgeon

Today, dare to place your hopes, your dreams, and your future in God's hands.

Who Are You?
You Are a Person Who Trusts God When Times Are Tough

For whatever is born of God overcomes the world.
And this is the victory that has overcome the world—our faith.
I John 5:4 NKJV

When we face tough times, God stands ready to protect us. All of us face times of adversity and stress. On occasion, we all must endure the disappointments and tragedies that befall believers and nonbelievers alike. The reassuring words of I John 5:4 remind us that when we accept God's grace, we overcome the passing hardships of this world by relying upon His strength, His love, and His promise of eternal life.

When we call upon God in heartfelt prayer, He will answer—in His own time and according to His own plan—and He will heal us. And while we are waiting for God's plans to unfold and for His healing touch to restore us, we can be comforted in the knowledge that our Creator can overcome any obstacle, even if we cannot. Let us take God at His word, and let us trust Him today . . . and every day.

Adversity is always unexpected and unwelcomed.
It is an intruder and a thief, and yet in the hands of God,
adversity becomes the means through which
His supernatural power is demonstrated.

Charles Stanley

In order to realize the worth of the anchor,
we need to feel the stress of the storm.

Corrie ten Boom

You'll never know that God is all you need
until God is all you've got.

Rick Warren

God will not permit any troubles to come upon us
unless He has a specific plan by which great blessing can
come out of the difficulty.

Peter Marshall

If you're having tough times, don't hit the panic button and don't keep everything bottled up inside. Talk things over with your friends and family, and if necessary, find a counselor you can really trust. A second opinion (or, for that matter, a third, fourth, or fifth opinion) is usually helpful. So if your troubles seem overwhelming, be willing to seek outside help.

Who Are You?
You Are a Person Who Asks God for the Things You Need

You do not have because you do not ask.
James 4:2 HCSB

If you want to gain a better understanding of the person you are today (and the person you want to become tomorrow), ask God to help you figure things out.

How often do you ask God for His guidance and His wisdom? Occasionally? Intermittently? Whenever you experience a crisis? Hopefully not. Hopefully, you've acquired the habit of asking for God's assistance early and often. And hopefully, you have learned to seek His guidance in every aspect of your life.

Do you sincerely seek to know God's unfolding plans for you? If so, ask Him for direction, for protection, and for strength—and then keep asking Him every day that you live. Whatever your need, no matter how great or small, pray about it and have faith. God is not just near; He is here, and He's perfectly capable of answering your prayers. Now, it's up to you to ask.

When you ask God to do something, don't ask timidly;
put your whole heart into it.

Marie T. Freeman

We honor God by asking for great things when
they are a part of His promise. We dishonor Him and
cheat ourselves when we ask for molehills
where He has promised mountains.

Vance Havner

We get into trouble when we think we know what to do
and we stop asking God if we're doing it.

Stormie Omartian

Notice that we must ask. And we will sometimes
struggle to hear and struggle with what we hear.
But personally, it's worth it. I'm after the path of life—
and he alone knows it.

John Eldredge

If you want more from life, ask more from God. If you're seeking
a worthy goal, ask for God's help—and keep asking—until He
answers your prayers.

Who Are You?
You Are a Person Who Remembers
That Actions Speak Louder Than Words

For the kingdom of God is not in talk but in power.
I Corinthians 4:20 HCSB

The old saying is both familiar and true: actions speak louder than words. And as believers, we must beware: our actions should always give credence to the changes that Christ can make in the lives of those who walk with Him.

God calls upon each of us to act in accordance with His will and with respect for His commandments. If we are to be responsible believers, we must realize that it is never enough simply to hear the instructions of God; we must also live by them. And it is never enough to wait idly by while others do God's work here on earth; we, too, must act. Doing God's work is a responsibility that each of us must bear, and when we do, our loving Heavenly Father rewards our efforts with a bountiful harvest.

Do you seek God's peace and His blessings? Then obey Him. When you're faced with a difficult choice or a powerful temptation, seek God's counsel and trust the counsel He gives. Invite God into your heart and act in accordance with His commandments. When you do, you will be blessed today, tomorrow, and forever.

Every word we speak, every action we take,
has an effect on the totality of humanity.
No one can escape that privilege—or that responsibility.
Laurie Beth Jones

It is by acts and not by ideas that people live.
Harry Emerson Fosdick

Never fail to do something because you don't feel like it.
Sometimes you just have to do it now,
and you'll feel like it later.
Marie T. Freeman

Try as we might, we simply cannot escape the consequences of our actions. How we behave today has a direct impact on the rewards we will receive tomorrow. That's a lesson that we must teach our students by our words and our actions, but not necessarily in that order.

Who Are You?
You Are a Person Who Avoids
the Wrong Kind of Peer Pressure

Whoever walks with the wise will become wise;
whoever walks with fools will suffer harm.

Proverbs 13:20 NLT

Who you are depends, to a surprising extent, on the people you hang out with. Peer pressure can be good or bad, depending upon who your peers are and how they behave. If your friends encourage you to follow God's will and to obey His commandments, then you'll experience positive peer pressure, and that's a good thing. But, if your friends encourage you to do foolish things, then you're facing a different kind of peer pressure . . . and you'd better beware.

Do you want to feel good about yourself and your life? If so, here's a simple, proven strategy: go out and find friends who, by their words and their actions, will help you build the kind of life that's worth feeling good about.

Nothing can be more dangerous than keeping
wicked companions. They communicate the infection
of their vices to all who associate with them.

St. Jean Baptiste de la Salle

Choose the opposition of the whole world
rather than offend Jesus.

Thomas à Kempis

You'll probably end up behaving like your friends behave . . .
and if that's a scary thought,
it's time to make a new set of friends.

Criswell Freeman

When we are set free from the bondage of pleasing others,
when we are free from currying others' favor and others'
approval—then no one will be able to make us miserable
or dissatisfied. And then, if we know we have pleased God,
contentment will be our consolation.

Kay Arthur

If you're hanging out with friends who behave badly, you're
heading straight for trouble. To avoid negative consequences,
pick friends who avoid negative behaviors.

Who Are You?
You Are a Person Who Listens to Your Conscience

*Now the goal of our instruction is love from a pure heart,
a good conscience, and a sincere faith.*

I Timothy 1:5 HCSB

God gave you a conscience for a very good reason: to make your path conform to His will. Billy Graham correctly observed, "Most of us follow our conscience as we follow a wheelbarrow. We push it in front of us in the direction we want to go." To do so, of course, is a profound mistake. Yet all of us, on occasion, have failed to listen to the voice that God planted in our hearts, and all of us have suffered the stressful consequences of our actions.

Wise believers make it a practice to listen carefully to that quiet internal voice. Count yourself among that number. When your conscience speaks, listen and learn. In all likelihood, God is trying to get His message through. And in all likelihood, it is a message that you desperately need to hear.

Your conscience is your alarm system.
It's your protection.
Charles Stanley

It is neither safe nor prudent to do anything
against one's conscience.
Martin Luther

God desires that we become spiritually healthy enough
through faith to have a conscience
that rightly interprets the work of the Holy Spirit.
Beth Moore

A good conscience is a continual feast.
Francis Bacon

The more stressful the situation, the more carefully you should
listen to your conscience.

Who Are You?
You Are a Person Who Places a High Value on Your Talents

I remind you to keep ablaze the gift of God that is in you.
2 Timothy 1:6 HCSB

Want to figure out who you are? You can start by taking a long, hard look at the talents God has given you. And you can be sure that you have an array of talents that need to be refined. All people possess special gifts—bestowed from the Father above—and you are no exception. But, your gift is no guarantee of success; it must be cultivated—by you—or it will go unused . . . and God's gift to you will be squandered.

Today, make a promise to yourself that you will earnestly seek to discover the talents that God has given you. Then, nourish those talents and make them grow. Finally, vow to share your gifts with the world for as long as God gives you the power to do so. After all, the best way to say "Thank You" for God's gifts is to use them.

You are a unique blend of talents, skills, and gifts, which makes you an indispensable member of the body of Christ.

Charles Stanley

Natural abilities are like natural plants;
they need pruning by study.

Francis Bacon

You are the only person on earth who can use your ability.

Zig Ziglar

God has given you a unique set of talents
and opportunities—talents and opportunities
that can be built up or buried—and the choice
to build or bury is entirely up to you.

Criswell Freeman

Today, take time to think about ways you can convert your talents into results.

Who Are You?
You Are a Person Who Finds the Courage to Follow God

Be strong and courageous, and do the work.
Don't be afraid or discouraged, for the Lord God, my God,
is with you. He won't leave you or forsake you.

I Chronicles 28:20 HCSB

Every life (including yours) is an unfolding series of events: some fabulous, some not-so-fabulous, and some downright disheartening. When you reach the mountaintops of life, praising God is easy. But, when the storm clouds form overhead, your faith will be tested, sometimes to the breaking point. As a believer, you can take comfort in this fact: Wherever you find yourself, whether at the top of the mountain or the depths of the valley, God is there, and because He cares for you, you can live courageously.

Believing Christians have every reason to be courageous. After all, the ultimate battle has already been fought and won on the cross at Calvary. But, even dedicated followers of Christ may find their courage tested by the inevitable disappointments and tragedies that occur in the lives of believers and non-believers alike.

The next time you find your courage tested to the limit, remember that God is as near as your next breath, and remember that He is your shield and your strength; He is your protector and your deliverer. Call upon Him in your hour of need and then be comforted. Whatever your challenge, whatever your trouble, God can handle it. And will.

Down through the centuries, in times of trouble and trial,
God has brought courage to the hearts of those
who love Him. The Bible is filled with assurances of
God's help and comfort in every kind of trouble which might
cause fears to arise in the human heart. You can look ahead
with promise, hope, and joy.

Billy Graham

The truth of Christ brings assurance and so removes
the former problem of fear and uncertainty.

A. W. Tozer

Do not let Satan deceive you into being
afraid of God's plans for your life.

R. A. Torrey

Who Are You?
You Are a Person Who Avoids the Constant Critics

*Therefore encourage one another
and build each other up as you are already doing.*
I Thessalonians 5:11 HCSB

If you want to feel better about yourself, find friends who are willing to offer you a steady stream of encouragement. And while you're at it, steer clear of the ceaseless critics and the chronic fault-finders.

In the book of James, we are issued a clear warning: "Don't criticize one another, brothers" (4:11 Holman CSB). Undoubtedly, James understood the paralyzing power of chronic negativity, and so should you.

Negativity is highly contagious, and can be highly hazardous to your sense of self-worth. So do yourself a major-league favor: find friends who make you feel better about yourself, not worse. Make no mistake: You deserve friends like that . . . and they deserve to have an encouraging friend like you.

After one hour in heaven,
we shall be ashamed that we ever grumbled.

Vance Havner

The scrutiny we give other people should be for ourselves.

Oswald Chambers

Discouraged people, if they must be discouraged, ought,
at least, to keep their discouragements to themselves,
hidden away in the privacy of their own bosoms lest they
should discourage the hearts of their brethren.

Hannah Whitall Smith

Being critical of others, including God, is one way we try
to avoid facing and judging our own sins.

Warren Wiersbe

Whether you realize it or not, you're a unique individual, created by God, with special talents and one-of-a-kind opportunities. Is that how you see yourself? If not, it's time to correct your spiritual vision.

Who Are You?
You Are a Person Who Knows
It's Important to Make Wise Choices

Exercise your freedom by serving God,
not by breaking rules.
1 Peter 2:16 MSG

Okay, answer this question honestly: Do you behave differently because of your relationship with Jesus? Or do you behave in pretty much the same way that you would if you weren't a believer? Hopefully, the fact that you've invited Christ to reign over your heart means that you've made BIG changes in your thoughts and your actions.

Doing the right thing is not always easy, especially when you're tired or frustrated. But, doing the wrong thing almost always leads to trouble (and, eventually, to poor self-esteem).

So if you want to feel good about yourself, don't follow the crowd—follow Jesus. And keep following Him every day of your life.

Although our actions have nothing to do with gaining
our own salvation, they might be used by God to save
somebody else! What we do really matters,
and it can affect the eternities of people we care about.

Bill Hybels

Nobody is good by accident.
No man ever became holy by chance.

C. H. Spurgeon

Either God's Word keeps you from sin,
or sin keeps you from God's Word.

Corrie ten Boom

Never support an experience which does not have God
as its source and faith in God as its result.

Oswald Chambers

If you're not sure that it's the right thing to do, don't do it!
And if you're not sure that it's the truth, don't tell it.

Who Are You?
You Are a Person Who Stands Up for Your Beliefs

I know whom I have believed and am persuaded that He is able to guard what has been entrusted to me until that day.

2 Timothy 1:12 HCSB

In describing one's beliefs, actions are far better descriptors than words. Yet far too many of us spend more energy talking about our beliefs than living by them—with predictable consequences.

Is your life a picture book of your creed? Are your actions congruent with your beliefs? Are you willing to practice the philosophy that you preach? If so, you'll most certainly feel better about yourself.

Today and every day, make certain that your actions are guided by God's Word and by the conscience that He has placed in your heart. Don't treat your faith as if it were separate from your everyday life. Weave your beliefs into the very fabric of your day. When you do, God will honor your good works, and your good works will honor God.

I do not seek to understand that I may believe,
but I believe in order to understand.

St. Augustine

Belief is not the result of an intellectual act;
it is the result of an act of my will whereby
I deliberately commit myself.

Oswald Chambers

You may as well quit reading and hearing
the Word of God and give it to the devil
if you do not desire to live according to it.

Martin Luther

God's presence is with you, but you have to make a choice
to believe—and I mean, really believe—that this is true.
This conscious decision is your alone.

Bill Hybels

When you stand up for your beliefs—and when you follow
your conscience—you'll feel better about yourself. When you
don't, you won't.

Who Are You?
You Are a Person Who Understands the Need to Serve

*The greatest among you will be your servant.
Whoever exalts himself will be humbled,
and whoever humbles himself will be exalted.*
Matthew 23:11-12 HCSB

We live in a world that glorifies power, prestige, fame, and money. But the words of Jesus teach us that the most esteemed men and women in this world are not the self-congratulatory leaders of society but are instead the humblest of servants.

Are you willing to become a humble servant for Christ? Are you willing to pitch in and make the world a better place, or are you determined to keep all your blessings to yourself? The answers to these questions will determine the quality and the direction of your day and your life.

Today, you may feel the temptation to take more than you give. You may be tempted to withhold your generosity. Or you may be tempted to build yourself up in the eyes of your friends. Resist those temptations. Instead, serve your friends quietly and without fanfare. Find a need and fill it . . .

humbly. Lend a helping hand . . . anonymously. Share a word of kindness . . . with quiet sincerity. As you go about your daily activities, remember that the Savior of all humanity made Himself a servant, and we, as His followers, must do no less.

In the very place where God has put us,
whatever its limitations, whatever kind of work it may be,
we may indeed serve the Lord Christ.

Elisabeth Elliot

God wants us to serve Him with a willing spirit,
one that would choose no other way.

Beth Moore

Through our service to others,
God wants to influence our world for Him.

Vonette Bright

Whatever your age, whatever your circumstances, you can serve: Each stage of life's journey is a glorious opportunity to place yourself in the service of the One who is the Giver of all blessings.

Who Are You?
You Are a Person Who Reads the Bible Every Day

Your word is a lamp for my feet and a light on my path.

Psalm 119:105 HCSB

If you're serious about getting to know yourself better, you'll need to get to know God better, too. And if you want to know God better, then you'll need to be serious about studying the book He wrote.

The words of Matthew 4:4 remind us that, "Man shall not live by bread alone but by every word that proceedeth out of the mouth of God" (KJV). Have you established a passionate relationship with God's Holy Word? Hopefully so. After all, the Bible is a roadmap for life here on earth and for life eternal. And, as a believer who has been touched by God's grace, you are called upon to study God's Holy Word, to trust His Word, to follow its commandments, and to share its Good News with the world.

As believers, we must study the Bible and meditate upon its meaning for our lives. Otherwise, we deprive ourselves of a priceless gift from our Creator. God's Holy Word is, indeed, a transforming gift from the Father in heaven. That's why passionate believers must never live by bread alone . . .

If you want to know God as he speaks to you through the Bible, you should study the Bible daily, systematically, comprehensively, devotionally, and prayerfully.

James Montgomery Boice

The Lord Jesus, available to people much of the time, left them, sometimes a great while before day, to go up to the hills where He could commune in solitude with His Father.

Elisabeth Elliot

Jesus taught us by example to get out of the rat race and recharge our batteries.

Barbara Johnson

Quiet time is giving God your undivided attention for a predetermined amount of time for the purpose of talking to and hearing from Him.

Charles Stanley

As we journey through this life, Lord, help us always to consult the true roadmap: Your Holy Word. We know that when we turn our hearts and our thoughts to You, Father, You will lead us along the path that is right for us. Today, Dear Lord, let us know Your will and study Your Word so that we might understand Your plan for our lives. Amen

Who Are You?
You Are a Person Who Understands the Need to Be a Cheerful Christian

A cheerful heart has a continual feast.
Proverbs 15:15 HCSB

Few things in life are more sad, or, for that matter, more absurd, than the sight of a grumpy, out of sorts Christian. Christ promises us lives of abundance and joy, but He does not force His joy upon us. We must claim His joy for ourselves, and when we do, Jesus, in turn, fills our spirits with His power and His love.

How can we receive from Christ the joy that is rightfully ours? By giving Him what is rightfully His: our hearts and our souls.

When we earnestly commit ourselves to the Savior of mankind, when we place Jesus at the center of our lives and trust Him as our personal Savior, He will transform us, not just for today, but for all eternity. Then we, as God's children, can share Christ's joy and His message with a world that needs both.

Be assured, my dear friend, that it is no joy to God
in seeing you with a dreary countenance.
C. H. Spurgeon

Sour godliness is the devil's religion.
John Wesley

The people whom I have seen succeed best in life have
always been cheerful and hopeful people who went about
their business with a smile on their faces.
Charles Kingsley

Christ can put a spring in your step
and a thrill in your heart. Optimism and cheerfulness
are products of knowing Christ.
Billy Graham

Do you need a little cheering up? If so, find somebody else who
needs cheering up, too. Then, do your best to brighten that
person's day. When you do, you'll discover that cheering up
other people is a wonderful way to cheer yourself up, too!

Who Are You?
You Are a Person Who Shares
Your Burdens with God

If God is for us, who is against us?
Romans 8:31 HCSB

The Bible promises this: tough times are temporary but God's love is not—God's love endures forever. So what does that mean to you? Just this: From time to time, everybody faces hardships and disappointments, and so will you. And when tough times arrive, God always stands ready to protect you and to heal you. Your task is straightforward: you must share your burdens with Him.

As Corrie ten Boom observed, "Any concern that is too small to be turned into a prayer is too small to be made into a burden." Those are comforting words, especially in these difficult days.

Whatever the size of your challenges, God is big enough to handle them. Ask for His help today, with faith and with fervor. Instead of turning things over in your mind, turn them over to God in prayer. Instead of worrying about your next decision, ask God to lead the way. Cast your burdens upon the One who cannot be shaken, and rest assured that He always hears your prayers.

When you're enjoying the fulfillment and fellowship that inevitably accompanies authentic service, ministry is a joy. Instead of exhausting you, it energizes you; instead of burnout, you experience blessing.

Bill Hybels

God knows what each of us is dealing with. He knows our pressures. He knows our conflicts. And, He has made a provision for each and every one of them. That provision is Himself in the person of the Holy Spirit, dwelling in us and empowering us to respond rightly.

Kay Arthur

No matter what we are going through, no matter how long the waiting for answers, of one thing we may be sure. God is faithful. He keeps His promises. What He starts, He finishes . . . including His perfect work in us.

Gloria Gaither

When you invite the love of God into your heart, everything changes . . . including you.

Who Are You?
You Are a Person Who Understands the Importance of Fellowship

*So reach out and welcome one another to God's glory.
Jesus did it; now you do it!*
Romans 15:7 MSG

If you genuinely want to become the kind of person who experiences a closer relationship with God, you'll need to build closer relationships with godly people. That's why fellowship with likeminded believers should be an integral part of your life. Your association with fellow Christians should be uplifting, enlightening, encouraging, and (above all) consistent.

Are your friends the kind of people who encourage you to seek God's will and to obey God's Word? If so, you've chosen your friends wisely. And that's a good thing because when you choose friends who honor God, you'll find it easier to honor Him, too.

One of the ways God refills us after failure is through the blessing of Christian fellowship. Just experiencing the joy of simple activities shared with other children of God can have a healing effect on us.

Anne Graham Lotz

Brotherly love is still the distinguishing badge of every true Christian.

Matthew Henry

I hope you will find a few folks who walk with God to also walk with you through the seasons of your life.

John Eldredge

Real fellowship happens when people get honest about who they are and what is happening in their lives.

Rick Warren

Here is a short list of things God wants you to do: 1. Go to church. 2. Pay attention in church. 3. Support the church. 4. Enjoy the fellowship of the people you meet in church. End of sermon

Who Are You?
You Are a Person Who Talks
Respectfully to Yourself

*Give in to God, come to terms with him
and everything will turn out just fine.*
Job 22:21 MSG

What are you telling yourself about yourself? When you look in the mirror, are you staring back at your biggest booster or your harshest critic? If you can learn to give yourself the benefit of the doubt—if you can learn how to have constructive conversations with the person you see in the mirror—then your self-respect will tend to take care of itself. But, if you're constantly berating yourself—if you're constantly telling yourself that you can't measure up—then you'll find that self-respect is always in short supply.

Thoughts are intensely powerful things. Your thoughts have the power to lift you up or drag you down; they have the power to energize you or deplete you, to inspire you to greater accomplishments, or to make those accomplishments impossible.

The Bible teaches you to guard your thoughts against things that are hurtful or wrong (Proverbs 4:23). Yet sometimes you'll be tempted to let your thoughts to run wild, especially if those thoughts are of the negative variety.

If you've acquired the habit of thinking constructively about yourself and your circumstances, congratulations. But if you're mired in the mental quicksand of overly self-critical thoughts, it's time to change your thoughts . . . and your life.

I may have tasted peace, but to believe that the God of heaven and earth calls me beautiful—well, I think I could rest in that. If I truly knew that He was smitten with me, maybe I could take a deep breath, square my shoulders, and go out to face the world with confidence.

Angela Thomas

As you and I lay up for ourselves living, lasting treasures in Heaven, we come to the awesome conclusion that we ourselves are His treasure!

Anne Graham Lotz

Pay careful attention to the way that you evaluate yourself. And if you happen to be your own worst critic, it's time to reevaluate the way that you've been evaluating (got that?)

Who Are You?
You Are a Person Who Doesn't Make Excuses

People's own foolishness ruins their lives,
but in their minds they blame the Lord.

Proverbs 19:3 NCV

Excuses are everywhere . . . excellence is not. Whether you're a student or a corporate CEO, your work is a picture book of your priorities. So whatever your job description, it's up to you, and no one else, to become masterful at your craft. It's up to you to do your job right, and to do it right now.

Because we humans are such creative excuse-makers, all of the best excuses have already been taken—we've heard them all before.

So if you're wasting your time trying to concoct a new and improved excuse, don't bother. It's impossible. A far better strategy is this: do the work. Now. Then, let your excellent work speak loudly and convincingly for itself.

Replace your excuses with fresh determination.

Charles Swindoll

An excuse is only the skin of a reason stuffed with a lie.

Vance Havner

We need to stop focusing on our lacks and stop giving out
excuses and start looking at and listening to Jesus.

Anne Graham Lotz

Making up a string of excuses is usually
harder than doing the work.

Marie T. Freeman

Today, think of something important that you've been putting
off. Then think of the excuses you've used to avoid that
responsibility. Finally, ask yourself what you can do today to
finish the work you've been avoiding.

Who Are You?
You Are a Person Who Understands
That You Are Blessed

So think clearly and exercise self-control.
Look forward to the special blessings that will come
to you at the return of Jesus Christ.

1 Peter 1:13 NLT

Because we have been so richly blessed, we should make thanksgiving a habit, a regular part of our daily routines. But sometimes, amid the demands and obligations of everyday life, we may allow the interruptions and distractions of everyday life to interfere with the time we spend with God.

Have you counted your blessings today? And have you thanked God for them? Hopefully so. After all, God's gifts include your family, your friends, your talents, your opportunities, your possessions, and the priceless gift of eternal life. How glorious are these gifts . . . and God is responsible for every one of them.

So today, as you go about the duties of everyday life, pause and give thanks to the Creator. He deserves your praise, and you deserve the experience of praising Him.

Only through routine, regular exposure to God's Word
can you and I draw out the nutrition needed
to grow a heart of faith.

Elizabeth George

Nobody ever outgrows Scripture;
the book widens and deepens with our years.

C. H. Spurgeon

Jesus intended for us to be overwhelmed by the blessings of
regular days. He said it was the reason he had come:
"I am come that they might have life,
and that they might have it more abundantly."

Gloria Gaither

Get rich quick! Count your blessings!

Anonymous

Lord, I have more blessings than I can possibly count; make me
mindful of Your precious gifts. You have cared for me, Lord, and
You have saved me. I will give thanks and praise You always.
Today, let me share Your blessings with others, just as You first
shared them with me. Amen

Who Are You?
You Are a Person Who Celebrates Life

This is the day which the LORD has made;
let us rejoice and be glad in it.
Psalm 118:24 NASB

What is the best day to celebrate life? This one! Today and every day should be a time for celebration as we consider the Good News of God's gift: salvation through Jesus Christ.

What do you expect from the day ahead? Are you expecting God to do wonderful things, or are you living beneath a cloud of worry and doubt?

The familiar words of Psalm 118:24 remind us of a profound yet simple truth: God made this day . . . and we, as believers, should rejoice in His marvelous creation. For Christians, every day begins and ends with God and His Son. Christ came to this earth to give us abundant life and eternal salvation. We give thanks to our Maker when we treasure each day. So with no further delay, let the celebration begin!

All our life is a celebration for us; we are convinced, in fact, that God is always everywhere. We sing while we work . . . we pray while we carry out all life's other occupations.

St. Clement of Alexandria

Some of us seem so anxious about avoiding hell that we forget to celebrate our journey toward heaven.

Philip Yancey

Celebration is possible only through the deep realization that life and death are never found completely separate. Celebration can really come about only where fear and love, joy and sorrow, tears and smiles can exist together.

Henri Nouwen

Joy is the great note all throughout the Bible.

Oswald Chambers

If you don't feel like celebrating, start counting your blessings. Before long, you'll realize that you have plenty of reasons to celebrate.

Who Are You?
You Are a Person Who Doesn't Judge Others

Stop judging others, and you will not be judged.
Stop criticizing others, or it will all come back on you.
If you forgive others, you will be forgiven.
Luke 6:37 NLT

Here's something worth thinking about: If you judge other people harshly, God will judge you in the same fashion. But that's not all (thank goodness!). The Bible also promises that if you forgive others, you, too, will be forgiven. Have you developed the bad habit of behaving yourself like an amateur judge and jury, assigning blame and condemnation wherever you go? If so, it's time to grow up and obey God.

When it comes to judging everything and everybody, God doesn't need your help . . . and He doesn't want it. So the next time you're beset by the temptation to judge another human being's motives, catch yourself before you make that mistake. Don't be a judge; be a witness.

Christians think they are prosecuting
attorneys or judges, when, in reality,
God has called all of us to be witnesses.

Warren Wiersbe

Don't judge other people more harshly
than you want God to judge you.

Marie T. Freeman

Turn your attention upon yourself and beware of judging
the deeds of other men, for in judging others
a man labors vainly, often makes mistakes, and easily sins;
whereas, in judging and taking stock of himself he does
something that is always profitable.

Thomas à Kempis

Your ability to judge others requires a divine insight that you
simply don't have. So do everybody (including yourself) a
favor: don't judge.

Who Are You?
You Are a Person Who Makes Time Each Day for God

Be careful not to forget the Lord.
Deuteronomy 6:12 HCSB

Each day has 1,440 minutes—do you value your relationship with God enough to spend a few of those minutes with Him? He deserves that much of your time and more. But if you find that you're simply "too busy" for a daily chat with your Father in heaven, it's time to take a long, hard look at your priorities and your values.

If you've acquired the unfortunate habit of trying to "squeeze" God into the corners of your life, it's time to reshuffle the items on your to-do list by placing God first. God wants your undivided attention, not the leftovers of your day. So, if you haven't already done so, form the habit of spending quality time with your Creator. He deserves it . . . and so, for that matter, do you.

When a church member gets overactive
and public worship is neglected, his or her relationship
with God will be damaged.
Anne Ortlund

The foe of opportunity is preoccupation. Just when God
sends along a chance to turn a great victory for mankind,
some of us are too busy puttering around to notice it.
A. W. Tozer

Are you weak? Weary? Confused? Troubled? Pressured?
How is your relationship with God? Is it held in its place of
priority? I believe the greater the pressure,
the greater your need for time alone with Him.
Kay Arthur

Busyness is the great enemy of relationships.
Rick Warren

Do first things first, and keep your focus on high-priority
tasks. And remember this: your highest priority should be
your relationship with God and His Son.

Who Are You?
You Are a Person Who Remembers Christ's Love

For I am persuaded that neither death nor life,
nor angels nor rulers, nor things present, nor things to come,
nor powers, nor height, nor depth, nor any other created thing
will have the power to separate us from the love of God
that is in Christ Jesus our Lord!
Romans 8:38-39 HCSB

How much does Christ love us? More than we, as mere mortals, can comprehend. His love is perfect and steadfast. Even though we are imperfect and wayward, the Good Shepherd cares for us still. Even though we have fallen far short of the Father's commandments, Christ loves us with a power and depth that are beyond our understanding. The sacrifice that Jesus made upon the cross was made for each of us, and His love endures to the edge of eternity and beyond.

Christ's love changes everything, including your relationships. When you accept His gift of grace, you are transformed, not only for today, but also for all eternity.

Jesus is waiting patiently for you to invite Him into your heart. Please don't make Him wait a single minute longer.

He loved us not because we're lovable,
but because He is love.

C. S. Lewis

God expressed His love in sending
the Holy Spirit to live within us.

Charles Stanley

God is my heavenly Father. He loves me with
an everlasting love. The proof of that is the Cross.

Elisabeth Elliot

Jesus loves me! This I know, for the Bible tells me so.
Little ones to him belong; they are weak, but he is strong.
Yes, Jesus loves me! Yes, Jesus loves me! Yes, Jesus loves me!
The Bible tells me so.

Anna B. Warner and Susan Warner

Jesus loves you . . . His love is amazing, it's wonderful, and it's meant for you.

Who Are You?
You Are a Person Who Focuses on the Spiritual Stuff

For those whose lives are according to the flesh think about the things of the flesh, but those whose lives are according to the Spirit, about the things of the Spirit.

Romans 8:5 HCSB

Is Christ the focus of your life? Are you fired with enthusiasm for Him? Are you an energized Christian who allows God's Son to reign over every aspect of your day? Make no mistake: that's exactly what God intends for you to do.

God has given you the gift of eternal life through His Son. In response to God's priceless gift, you are instructed to focus your thoughts, your prayers, and your energies upon God and His only begotten Son. To do so, you must resist the subtle yet powerful temptation to become a "spiritual dabbler."

A person who dabbles in the Christian faith is unwilling to place God in His rightful place: above all other things. Resist that temptation; make God the cornerstone and the touchstone of your life—including your dating life. When you do, He will give you all the strength and wisdom you need to live victoriously for Him.

Whatever we focus on determines what we become.

E. Stanley Jones

Blessed are those who know what on earth they are
here on earth to do and set themselves
about the business of doing it.

Max Lucado

Jesus. If you are walking toward him to the best of your
ability, he will see you through life's unpredictable waters—
but you must risk launching the boat.

Patsy Clairmont

The Christian lifestyle is not one of legalistic do's and don'ts,
but one that is positive, attractive, and joyful.

Vonette Bright

First focus on God . . . and then everything else will come into
focus.

Who Are You?
You Are a Person Who Doesn't Let Failures Get You Down

Though a righteous man falls seven times, he will get up,
but the wicked will stumble into ruin.

Proverbs 24:16 HCSB

The occasional disappointments and failures of life are inevitable. Such setbacks are simply the price that we must occasionally pay for our willingness to take risks as we follow our dreams. But even when we encounter bitter disappointments, we must never lose faith.

The reassuring words of Hebrews 10:36 remind us that when we persevere, we will eventually receive that which God has promised. What's required is perseverance, not perfection.

When we encounter the inevitable difficulties and stresses of life here on earth, God stands ready to protect us. Our responsibility, of course, is to ask Him for protection. When we call upon Him in heartfelt prayer, He will answer—in His own time and according to His own plan—and He will heal us. And, while we are waiting for God's plans to unfold and for His healing touch to restore us, we can be comforted in the knowledge that our Creator can overcome any obstacle, even if we cannot.

We become a failure when we allow mistakes to take away our ability to learn, give, grow, and try again.

Susan Lenzkes

If you're willing to repair your life, God is willing to help. If you're not willing to repair your life, God is willing to wait.

Marie T. Freeman

God is a specialist; He is well able to work our failures into His plans. Often the doorway to success is entered through the hallway of failure.

Erwin Lutzer

If you learn from a defeat, you have not really lost.

Zig Ziglar

Failure isn't permanent . . . unless you fail to get back up. So pick yourself up, dust yourself off, and trust God. Warren Wiersbe had this advice: "No matter how badly we have failed, we can always get up and begin again. Our God is the God of new beginnings." And don't forget: the best time to begin again is now.

Who Are You?
You Are a Person Who Seeks Strength from God

The Lord is my strength and my song;
He has become my salvation.

Exodus 15:2 HCSB

Where do you go to find strength? The gym? The health food store? The espresso bar? There's a better source of strength, of course, and that source is God. He is a never-ending source of strength and courage if you call upon Him.

Have you "tapped in" to the power of God? Have you turned your life, your relationships, and your heart over to Him—or are you muddling along under your own power? The answer to this question will determine the quality of your life here on earth and the destiny of your life throughout all eternity. So start tapping in—and remember that when it comes to strength, God is the Ultimate Source.

Sometimes I think spiritual and physical strength
is like manna: you get just what you need
for the day, no more.

Suzanne Dale Ezell

When God is our strength, it is strength indeed;
when our strength is our own, it is only weakness.

St. Augustine

When we reach the end of our strength, wisdom,
and personal resources, we enter into the beginning
of his glorious provisions.

Patsy Clairmont

God is great and God is powerful, but we must invite him
to be powerful in our lives. His strength is always there,
but it's up to us to provide a channel through
which that power can flow.

Bill Hybels

If you're energy is low or your nerves are frazzled, perhaps you
need to slow down and have a heart-to-heart talk with God.
And while you're at it, remember that God is bigger than your
problems . . . much bigger.

Who Are You?
You Are a Person Who Doesn't Hang Out with Cruel People

Dear friend, do not imitate what is evil, but what is good.
The one who does good is of God;
the one who does evil has not seen God.

3 John 1:11 HCSB

Face it: sometimes people can be very cruel. And when people are unkind to you or to your friends, you may be tempted to strike back in anger. Don't do it! Instead, remember that God corrects other people's behaviors in His own way, and He doesn't need your help. And remember that God has commanded you to forgive others, just as you, too, must sometimes seek forgiveness from them.

So, when other people are cruel, as they most certainly will be from time to time, what should you do? 1. Politely speak up for yourself (and for people who can't speak up for themselves), 2. Forgive everybody as quickly as you can, 3. Leave the rest up to God, and 4. Move on with your life by making sure that you don't consistently hang out with cruel people.

Pride opens the door to every other sin,
for once we are more concerned with our reputation
than our character, there is no end to the things
we will do just to make ourselves
"look good" before others.

Warren Wiersbe

Sour godliness is the devil's religion.

John Wesley

Good will is written into the constitution of things;
ill will is sand in the machinery.

E. Stanley Jones

The attitude of kindness is everyday stuff like
a great pair of sneakers. Not frilly. Not fancy.
Just plain and comfortable.

Barbara Johnson

A thoughtful Christian doesn't follow the crowd . . . a
thoughtful Christian follows Jesus.

Who Are You?
You Are a Person Who Knows
It's Important to Control Your Temper

When you are angry, do not sin, and be sure to stop
being angry before the end of the day.
Do not give the devil a way to defeat you.
Ephesians 4:26–27 NCV

The frustrations of everyday living can sometimes get the better of us, and we allow minor disappointments to cause us major problems. When we allow ourselves to become overly irritated by the inevitable ups and downs of life, we become overstressed, overheated, overanxious, and just plain angry.

As the old saying goes, "Anger usually improves nothing but the arch of a cat's back." So don't allow feelings of anger or frustration to rule your life, or, for that matter, your day—your life is simply too short for that, and you deserve much better treatment than that . . . from yourself.

When you strike out in anger, you may miss the other person, but you will always hit yourself.

Jim Gallery

Life is too short to spend it being angry, bored, or dull.

Barbara Johnson

Anger unresolved will only bring you woe.

Kay Arthur

Is there somebody who's always getting your goat? Talk to the Shepherd.

Anonymous

If you think you're about to be overcome with anger, pitch a fit, or throw a tantrum, slow down, catch your breath, and walk away if you must. It's better to walk away (and keep walking) than it is to blurt out angry words that can't be un-blurted.

Who Are You?
You Are a Person Who Understands the Importance of Silence

Be still, and know that I am God.
Psalm 46:10 NKJV

The Bible teaches that a wonderful way to get to know God is simply to be still and listen to Him. But sometimes, you may find it hard to slow down and listen.

As the demands of everyday life weigh down upon you, you may be tempted to ignore God's presence or—worse yet—to rebel against His commandments. But, when you quiet yourself and acknowledge His presence, God touches your heart and restores your spirits. So why not let Him do it right now? If you really want to know Him better, silence is a wonderful place to start.

Instead of waiting for the feeling, wait upon God.
You can do this by growing still and quiet, then expressing
in prayer what your mind knows is true about Him,
even if your heart doesn't feel it at this moment.

Shirley Dobson

When we are in the presence of God, removed from
distractions, we are able to hear him more clearly,
and a secure environment has been established for the young
and broken places in our hearts to surface.

John Eldredge

I have come to recognize that He never asks us to do
anything He has not already done. He never takes us anyplace
where He has not been ahead of us. What He is after is not
performance, but a relationship with us.

Gloria Gaither

Want to talk to God? Then don't make Him shout. If you really
want to hear from God, go to a quiet place and listen. If you
keep listening long enough and carefully enough, He'll start
talking.

Who Are You?
You Are a Person Who Understands It's Important to Be Involved in a Church

And I also say to you that you are Peter, and on this rock I will build My church, and the forces of Hades will not overpower it. I will give you the keys of the kingdom of heaven, and whatever you bind on earth will have been bound in heaven, and whatever you loose on earth will have been loosed in heaven.
Matthew 16:18-19 HCSB

A good way to figure out the kind of person you want to become is by worshiping with people who love and respect you. That's one reason (but certainly not the only reason) that you should be an active member of a supportive congregation.

Every believer—including you—needs to be part of a community of faith. Your association with fellow Christians should be uplifting, enlightening, encouraging, and consistent.

Are you an active member of your fellowship? Are you a builder of bridges inside the four walls of your church and outside it? Do you contribute your time and your talents to a close-knit band of hope-filled believers? Hopefully so. The fellowship of believers is intended to be a powerful tool for spreading God's Good News and uplifting His children. God intends for you to be a fully contributing member of that fellowship. Your intentions should be the same.

The church has no greater need today
than to fall in love with Jesus all over again.
Vance Havner

Only participation in the full life of a local church builds
spiritual muscle.
Rick Warren

The Bible knows nothing of solitary religion.
John Wesley

If you become a fully participating member of an active congregation, you'll become more excited about your faith, your world, and yourself. So do yourself a favor: be an active member of your fellowship.

Who Are You?
You Are a Person Who Isn't Too Attached to the World

Don't love the world's ways. Don't love the world's goods. Love of the world squeezes out love for the Father. Practically everything that goes on in the world—wanting your own way, wanting everything for yourself, wanting to appear important— has nothing to do with the Father. It just isolates you from him. The world and all its wanting, wanting, wanting is on the way out—but whoever does what God wants is set for eternity.

1 John 2:15-17 MSG

Our world is filled with pressures: some good, some bad. The pressures that we feel to follow God's will and obey His commandments are positive pressures. God places them on our hearts so that we might act in accordance with His will. But we also face different pressures, ones that are definitely not from God. When we feel pressured to do things—or even to think thoughts—that lead us away from Him, we must beware.

Many elements of society seek to mold us into more worldly beings; God, on the other hand, seeks to mold us into new beings, new creations through Christ, beings that are most certainly not conformed to this world. If we are to please God, we must resist the pressures that society seeks to impose upon us, and we must conform ourselves, instead, to His will, to His path, and to His Son.

The only ultimate disaster that can befall us, I have come to realize, is to feel ourselves to be home on earth.
Max Lucado

The true Christian, though he is in revolt against the world's efforts to brainwash him, is no mere rebel for rebellion's sake. He dissents from the world because he knows that it cannot make good on its promises.
A. W. Tozer

The more we stuff ourselves with material pleasures, the less we seem to appreciate life.
Barbara Johnson

The world makes plenty of promises that it can't keep. God, on the other hand, keeps every single one of His promises.

Who Are You?
You Are a Person Who Keeps Your Fears in Perspective

*They won't be afraid of bad news;
their hearts are steady because they trust the Lord.*

Psalm 112:7 NCV

His adoring fans called him the "Sultan of Swat." He was Babe Ruth, the baseball player who set records for home runs and strikeouts. Babe's philosophy was simple. He said, "Never let the fear of striking out get in your way." That's smart advice on the diamond or off.

Of course it's never wise to take foolish risks (so buckle up, slow down, and don't do anything silly). But when it comes to the game of life, you should not let the fear of failure keep you from taking your swings.

Today, ask God for the courage to step beyond the boundaries of your self-doubts. Ask Him to guide you to a place where you can realize your full potential—a place where you are freed from the fear of failure. Ask Him to do His part, and promise Him that you will do your part. Don't ask Him to lead you to a "safe" place; ask Him to lead you to the "right" place . . . and remember: those two places are seldom the same.

Earthly fears are no fears at all.
Answer the big question of eternity,
and the little questions of life fall into perspective.

Max Lucado

I have found the perfect antidote for fear.
Whenever it sticks up its ugly face,
I clobber it with prayer.

Dale Evans Rogers

When once we are assured that God is good,
then there can be nothing left to fear.

Hannah Whitall Smith

Call upon God. Prayer itself can defuse fear.

Bill Hybels

Are you feeling anxious or fearful? If so, trust God to handle those problems that are simply too big for you to solve. Entrust the future—your future—to God. Then, spend a few minutes thinking about specific steps you can take to confront—and conquer—your fears.

Who Are You?
You Are a Person Who Understands the Need to Be a Good Communicator

Rash language cuts and maims,
but there is healing in the words of the wise.
Proverbs 12:18 MSG

If you want to build strong relationships, you should teach yourself to become an effective communicator. And that's exactly what God wants you to do. God's Word reminds us that "Reckless words pierce like a sword, but the tongue of the wise brings healing" (Proverbs 12:18 NIV).

Today, make this promise to yourself: vow to be an honest, effective, encouraging communicator at school, at home, at church, and everyplace in between. Speak wisely, not impulsively. Use words of kindness and praise, not words of anger or derision. Learn how to be truthful without being cruel. Remember that you have the power to heal others or to injure them, to lift others up or to hold them back. And when you learn how to lift them up, you'll soon discover that you've lifted yourself up, too.

Happy the man whose words issue
from the Holy Spirit and not from himself.

Anthony of Padua

Like dynamite, God's power is only latent power
until it is released. You can release God's dynamite power
into people's lives and the world through faith,
your words, and prayer.

Bill Bright

Attitude and the spirit in which we communicate
are as important as the words we say.

Charles Stanley

Part of good communication is listening
with the eyes as well as with the ears.

Josh McDowell

Think First, Speak Second: If you blurt out the first thing that comes into your head, you may say things that are better left unsaid.

Who Are You?
You Are a Person Who Treats Your Body with Respect

*Don't you know that you are God's temple
and that God's Spirit lives in you?*

1 Corinthians 3:16 NCV

One of the quickest ways to destroy your self-esteem is to start treating your body with disrespect.

How do you treat your body? Do you treat it with the reverence and respect it deserves, or do you take it more or less for granted? Well, the Bible has clear instructions about the way you should take care of the miraculous body that God has given you.

God's Word teaches us that our bodies are "temples" that belong to God (1 Corinthians 6:19-20). We are commanded (not encouraged, not advised—we are commanded!) to treat our bodies with respect and honor. We do so by making wise choices and by making those choices consistently over an extended period of time.

Do you sincerely seek to improve the overall quality of your life and your health? Then promise yourself—and God—that you will begin making the kind of wise choices that will lead to a longer, healthier, happier life. The responsibility for those choices is yours. And so are the rewards.

God wants you to give Him your body.
Some people do foolish things with their bodies.
God wants your body as a holy sacrifice.

Warren Wiersbe

People are funny. When they are young,
they will spend their health to get wealth.
Later, they will gladly pay all they have trying
to get their health back.

John Maxwell

Our body is a portable sanctuary through which
we are daily experiencing the presence of God.

Richard Foster

The Creator has made us each one of a kind. There is nobody
else exactly like us, and there never will be. Each of us is his
special creation and is alive for a distinctive purpose.

Luci Swindoll

God has given you a marvelous gift: your body. Taking care of
that body is your responsibility. Don't dodge that responsibility!
Give your body the respect it deserves.

Who Are You?
You Are a Person Who Makes Smart Choices

*But the wisdom from above is first pure, then peace-loving,
gentle, compliant, full of mercy and good fruits,
without favoritism and hypocrisy.*

James 3:17 HCSB

Because we are creatures of free will, we make choices—lots of them. When we make choices that are pleasing to our Heavenly Father, we are blessed. When we make choices that cause us to walk in the footsteps of God's Son, we enjoy the abundance that Christ has promised to those who follow Him. But when you make choices that are displeasing to God, we sow seeds that have the potential to bring forth a bitter, stressful harvest.

Today, as you encounter the challenges of everyday living, you will make hundreds of choices. Choose wisely. Make your thoughts and your actions pleasing to God. And remember: every choice that is displeasing to Him is the wrong choice—no exceptions.

We are either the masters or the victims of our attitudes. It is a matter of personal choice. Who we are today is the result of choices we made yesterday. Tomorrow, we will become what we choose today. To change means to choose to change.

John Maxwell

Good and evil both increase at compound interest. That is why the little decisions you and I make every day are of such infinite importance.

C. S. Lewis

God expresses His love in giving us the freedom to choose.

Charles Stanley

Life is a series of choices between the bad, the good, and the best. Everything depends on how we choose.

Vance Havner

Wise choices bring you happiness; unwise choices don't. So whenever you have a choice to make, choose wisely and prayerfully.

Who Are You?
You Are a Person Who Doesn't Overestimate the Importance of Appearances

As the water reflects the face, so the heart reflects the person.
Proverbs 27:19 HCSB

The world sees you as you appear to be; God sees you as you really are. He sees your heart, and He understands your intentions. The opinions of others should be relatively unimportant to you; however, God's view of you—His understanding of your actions, your thoughts, and your motivations—should be vitally important.

Few things in life are more futile than "keeping up appearances" in order to impress your friends and your dates—yet the media would have you believe otherwise. The media would have you believe that everything depends on the color of your hair, the condition of your wardrobe, and the model of the car you drive. But nothing could be further from the truth. What is important, of course, is pleasing your Father in heaven. You please Him when your intentions are pure and your actions are just. When you do, you will be blessed today, tomorrow, and forever.

Outside appearances, things like the clothes you wear
or the car you drive, are important to other people but
totally unimportant to God. Trust God.

Marie T. Freeman

The temptation of the age is to look good
without being good.

Brennan Manning

If the narrative of the Scriptures teaches us anything,
from the serpent in the Garden to the carpenter in Nazareth,
it teaches us that things are rarely what they seem,
that we shouldn't be fooled by appearances.

John Eldredge

Too many Christians have geared their program to please,
to entertain, and to gain favor from this world.
We are concerned with how much, instead of how little,
like this age we can become.

Billy Graham

When making judgments about friends and dates, don't focus
on appearances, focus on values.

Who Are You?
You Are a Person Who
Doesn't Get Discouraged

But as for you, be strong; don't be discouraged,
for your work has a reward.

2 Chronicles 15:7 HCSB

We Christians have many reasons to celebrate. God is in His heaven; Christ has risen, and we are the sheep of His flock. Yet sometimes, even the most devout Christians can become discouraged. After all, we live in a world where expectations can be high and demands can be even higher. If you become discouraged with the direction of your day or your life, turn your thoughts and prayers to God. He is a God of possibility, not negativity. He will help you count your blessings instead of your hardships. And then, with a renewed spirit of optimism and hope, you can properly thank your Father in heaven for His blessings, for His love, and for His Son.

Overcoming discouragement is simply a matter of
taking away the DIS and adding the EN.

Barbara Johnson

The Christian life is not a constant high.
I have my moments of deep discouragement.
I have to go to God in prayer with tears in my eyes, and say,
"O God, forgive me," or "Help me."

Billy Graham

The most profane word we use is "hopeless."
When you say a situation or person is hopeless,
you are slamming the door in the face of God.

Kathy Troccoli

All discouragement is of the devil.

Hannah Whitall Smith

When things go wrong, it's easy to become discouraged. But
those who follow Jesus need never be discouraged because
God's promises are true . . . and heaven is eternal.

Who Are You?
You Are a Person Who
Shines Your Light

It is God's will that your good lives should silence those
who make foolish accusations against you. You are not slaves;
you are free. But your freedom is not an excuse to do evil.
You are free to live as God's slaves.

1 Peter 2:15-16 NLT

All of us are examples—examples that should be emulated . . . or not. Hopefully, the lives we lead and the choices we make will serve as enduring examples of the spiritual abundance that is available to all who worship God and obey His commandments.

Ask yourself this question: Are you the kind of role model that you would want to emulate? If so, congratulations. But if certain aspects of your behavior could stand improvement, the best day to begin your self-improvement regimen is this one. Because whether you realize it or not, people you love are watching your behavior, and they're learning how to live. You owe it to them—and to yourself—to live righteously and well.

Living life with a consistent spiritual walk
deeply influences those we love most.

Vonette Bright

We urgently need people who encourage
and inspire us to move toward God and away from
the world's enticing pleasures.

Jim Cymbala

In our faith we follow in someone's steps.
In our faith we leave footprints to guide others.
It's the principle of discipleship.

Max Lucado

The sermon of your life in tough times ministers to people
more powerfully than the most eloquent speaker.

Bill Bright

Your life is a sermon. What kind of sermon will you preach?
The words you choose to speak may have some impact on
others, but not nearly as much impact as the life you choose
to live.

Who Are You?
You Are a Person Who Follows Christ

"Follow Me," Jesus told them, "and I will make you into fishers of men!" Immediately they left their nets and followed Him.
Mark 1:17-18 HCSB

Can you honestly say that you're passionate about your faith and that you're really following Jesus? Hopefully so. But if you're preoccupied with other things—or if you're strictly a one-day-a-week Christian—then you're in need of a major-league spiritual makeover.

Jesus doesn't want you to be a lukewarm believer; Jesus wants you to be a "new creation" through Him. And that's exactly what you should want for yourself, too. Nothing is more important than your wholehearted commitment to your Creator and to His only begotten Son. Your faith must never be an afterthought; it must be your ultimate priority, your ultimate possession, and your ultimate passion.

You are the recipient of Christ's love. Accept it enthusiastically and share it passionately. Jesus deserves your undivided attention. And when you give it to Him, you'll be forever grateful that you did.

Christ is like a river that is continually flowing.
There are always fresh supplies of water coming from
the fountain-head, so that a man may live by it and be
supplied with water all his life. So Christ is an ever-flowing
fountain; he is continually supplying his people,
and the fountain is not spent. They who live upon Christ
may have fresh supplies from him for all eternity; they may
have an increase of blessedness that is new, and new still,
and which never will come to an end.

Jonathan Edwards

Jesus challenges you and me to keep our focus daily on
the cross of His will if we want to be His disciples.

Anne Graham Lotz

It's your heart that Jesus longs for:
your will to be made His own with self on the cross forever,
and Jesus alone on the throne.

Ruth Bell Graham

Remember that God blesses those who choose to follow
Christ. Jesus is ready to lead you; it's up to you to follow.

Who Are You?
You Are a Person Who Understands the Need to Be Generous

The good person is generous and lends lavishly . . . .
Psalm 112:5 MSG

D o you want to improve your self-esteem? Then make sure that you're a generous person. When you give generously to those who need your help, God will bless your endeavors and enrich your life. So, if you're looking for a surefire way to improve the quality of your day or your life, here it is: find ways to share your blessings.

God rewards generosity just as surely as He punishes sin. If we become generous disciples in the service of our Lord, God blesses us in ways that we cannot fully understand. But if we allow ourselves to become closefisted and miserly, either with our possessions or with our love, we deprive ourselves of the spiritual abundance that would otherwise be ours.

Do you seek God's abundance and His peace? Then share the blessings that God has given you. Share your possessions, share your faith, share your testimony, and share your love. God expects no less, and He deserves no less. And neither, come to think of it, do your neighbors.

He climbs highest who helps another up.

Zig Ziglar

Anything done for another is done for oneself.

Pope John Paul II

The mind grows by taking in,
but the heart grows by giving out.

Warren Wiersbe

If there be any truer measure of a man
than by what he does, it must be by what he gives.

Robert South

Generosity 101: Some of the best stuff you'll ever have is the stuff you give away.

Who Are You?
You Are a Person Who
Stays Humble

Therefore humble yourselves under the mighty hand of God,
that He may exalt you in due time.

I Peter 5:6 NKJV

On the road to spiritual growth, pride is a massive roadblock. The more prideful you are, the more difficult it is to know God. When you experience success, it's easy to puff out your chest and proclaim, "I did that!" But it's wrong. Dietrich Bonhoeffer was correct when he observed, "It is very easy to overestimate the importance of our own achievements in comparison with what we owe others." In other words, reality breeds humility. So if you want to know God better, be humble. Otherwise, you'll be building a roadblock between you and your Creator (and that's a very bad thing to do!).

Do you wish to rise? Begin by descending.
You plan a tower that will pierce the clouds?
Lay first the foundation of humility.

St. Augustine

The great characteristic of the saint is humility.

Oswald Chambers

Nothing sets a person so much out of the devil's reach as
humility.

Jonathan Edwards

Yes, we need to acknowledge our weaknesses, to confess
our sins. But if we want to be active, productive participants
in the realm of God, we also need to recognize our gifts,
to appreciate our strengths, to build on the abilities God has
given us. We need to balance humility with confidence.

Penelope Stokes

Do you value humility above status? If so, God will smile upon
your endeavors. But if you value status above humility, you're
inviting God's displeasure. In short, humility pleases God;
pride does not.

Who Are You?
You Are a Person Who
Pays Attention to God

Your heart will be where your treasure is.
Luke 12:34 NCV

Jesus deserves your undivided attention. Are you giving it to Him? Hopefully so.

When you focus your thoughts and prayers on the One from Galilee, you'll start building a better life and better relationships. But beware: the world will try to convince you that "other things" are more important than your faith. These messages are both false and dangerous—don't believe them.

When it comes to your spiritual, emotional, and personal growth, absolutely nothing is more important than your faith. So do yourself and your loved ones a favor: focus on God and His only begotten Son. Your loved ones will be glad you did . . . and so will you.

He doesn't need an abundance of words.
He doesn't need a dissertation about your life.
He just wants your attention. He wants your heart.

Kathy Troccoli

Make a plan now to keep a daily appointment with God.
The enemy is going to tell you to set it aside, but you must
carve out the time. If you're too busy to meet with the Lord,
friend, then you are simply too busy.

Charles Swindoll

If we really believe not only that God exists but also
that God is actively present in our lives—healing, teaching,
and guiding—we need to set aside a time and space
to give God our undivided attention.

Henri Nouwen

If you, too, will learn to wait upon God, to get alone
with Him, and remain silent so that you can hear His voice
when He is ready to speak to you,
what a difference it will make in your life!

Kay Arthur

The world wants you to focus on "stuff." God wants you to
focus on His Son. Trust God.

Who Are You?
You Are a Person Who
Seeks God's Guidance

The true children of God are those
who let God's Spirit lead them.
Romans 8:14 NCV

The Bible promises that God will guide you if you let Him. Your job is to let Him. But sometimes, you will be tempted to do otherwise. Sometimes, you'll be tempted to go along with the crowd; other times, you'll be tempted to do things your way, not God's way. When you feel these temptations, resist them.

God has promised that when you ask for His help, He will not withhold it. So ask. Ask Him to meet the needs of your day. Ask Him to lead you, to protect you, and to correct you. And trust the answers He gives.

God stands at the door and waits. When you knock, He opens. When you ask, He answers. Your task, of course, is to seek His guidance prayerfully, confidently, and often.

We have ample evidence that the Lord is able to guide.
The promises cover every imaginable situation.
All we need to do is to take the hand he stretches out.

Elisabeth Elliot

Only He can guide you to invest your life in worthwhile
ways. This guidance will come as you "walk"
with Him and listen to Him.

Henry Blackaby and Claude King

Are you serious about wanting God's guidance
to become a personal reality in your life?
The first step is to tell God that you know you can't manage
your own life; that you need his help.

Catherine Marshall

If we want to hear God's voice,
we must surrender our minds and hearts to Him.

Billy Graham

Is God your spare wheel or your steering wheel? Let God guide
your way.

Who Are You?
You Are a Person Who Tries to See Things from God's Perspective

All I'm doing right now, friends, is showing how these things pertain to Apollos and me so that you will learn restraint and not rush into making judgments without knowing all the facts. It is important to look at things from God's point of view. I would rather not see you inflating or deflating reputations based on mere hearsay.

I Corinthians 4:6 MSG

Sometimes, amid the demands of daily life, we lose perspective. Life seems out of balance, and the pressures of everyday living seem overwhelming. What's needed is a fresh perspective, a restored sense of balance . . . and God. If we call upon the Lord and seek to see the world through His eyes, He will give us guidance and wisdom and perspective. When we make God's priorities our priorities, He will lead us according to His plan and according to His commandments. God's reality is the ultimate reality. May we live accordingly.

Like a shadow declining swiftly . . . away . . . like the dew
of the morning gone with the heat of the day; like the wind
in the treetops, like a wave of the sea, so are our lives
on earth when seen in light of eternity.

Ruth Bell Graham

The Bible is a remarkable commentary on perspective.
Through its divine message, we are brought face to face
with issues and tests in daily living and how,
by the power of the Holy Spirit, we are enabled
to respond positively to them.

Luci Swindoll

We forget that God sometimes has to say "No."
We pray to Him as our heavenly Father, and like wise
human fathers, He often says, "No," not from whim or
caprice, but from wisdom, from love,
and from knowing what is best for us.

Peter Marshall

Keep life in perspective: Your life is an integral part of God's
grand plan. So don't become unduly upset over the minor
inconveniences of life, and don't worry too much about today's
setbacks—they're temporary.

Who Are You?
You Are a Person Who Understands That God Is Always Present

The Lord is with you when you are with Him.
If you seek Him, He will be found by you.
2 Chronicles 15:2 HCSB

D o you ever wonder if God is really "right here, right now"? Do you wonder if God hears your prayers, if He understands your feelings, or if He really knows your heart? If so, you're not alone: lots of very faithful Christians have experienced periods of doubt. In fact, some of the biggest heroes in the Bible had plenty of doubts—and so, perhaps, will you. But when you have doubts, remember this: God isn't on a coffee break, and He hasn't moved out of town. He's right here, right now, listening to your thoughts and prayers, watching over your every move.

If you'd like to get to know God a little bit better, He's always available—always ready to listen to your prayers, and always ready to speak to your heart. Are you ready to talk to Him? If so, congratulations. If not, what are you waiting for?

Our body is a portable sanctuary through which
we are daily experiencing the presence of God.

Richard Foster

The tender eyes of God perpetually see us.
He has never stopped noticing.

Angela Thomas

God's presence is with you, but you have to make
a choice to believe—and I mean, really believe—
that this is true. This conscious decision is your alone.

Bill Hybels

God expresses His love toward us by His uninterrupted
presence in our lives.

Charles Stanley

God isn't far away—He's right here, right now. And He's
willing to talk to you right here, right now.

Who Are You?
You Are a Person Who Trusts God's Promises

God—His way is perfect; the word of the Lord is pure.
He is a shield to all who take refuge in Him.

Psalm 18:30 HCSB

What do you expect from the day ahead? Are you willing to trust God completely, or are you living beneath a cloud of doubt and fear? God's Word makes it clear: you should trust Him and His promises, and when you do, you can live courageously.

For thoughtful Christians, every day begins and ends with God's Son and God's promises. When we accept Christ into our hearts, God promises us the opportunity for earthly peace and spiritual abundance. But more importantly, God promises us the priceless gift of eternal life.

Sometimes, especially when we find ourselves caught in the inevitable entanglements of life, we fail to trust God completely.

Are you tired? Discouraged? Fearful? Be comforted and trust the promises that God has made to you. Are you worried or stressed? Be confident in God's power. Do you see a difficult future ahead? Be courageous and call upon God. He will protect you and then use you according to His purposes. Are you confused? Listen to the quiet voice of your Heavenly Father. He is not a God of confusion. Talk with Him; listen to Him; trust Him, and trust His promises. He is steadfast, and He is your Protector . . . forever.

God's promises are medicine for the broken heart.
Let Him comfort you. And, after He has comforted you,
try to share that comfort with somebody else.
It will do both of you good.
Warren Wiersbe

We can have full confidence in God's promises
because we can have full faith in His character.
Franklin Graham

In Biblical worship you do not find the repetition of a phrase;
instead, you find the worshipers rehearsing the character
of God and His ways, reminding Him of
His faithfulness and His wonderful promises.
Kay Arthur

Who Are You?
You Are a Person Who Understands the Value of a Positive Attitude

Finally brothers, whatever is true, whatever is honorable, whatever is just, whatever is pure, whatever is lovely, whatever is commendable—if there is any moral excellence and if there is any praise—dwell on these things.

Philippians 4:8 HCSB

How will you direct your thoughts today? Will you obey the words of Philippians 4:8 by dwelling upon those things that are honorable, just, and commendable? Or will you allow your thoughts to be hijacked by the negativity that seems to dominate our troubled world? Are you fearful, angry, stressed, or worried? Are you so preoccupied with the concerns of this day that you fail to thank God for the promise of eternity? Are you confused, bitter, or pessimistic? If so, God wants to have a little talk with you.

God intends that you experience joy and abundance. So, today and every day hereafter, celebrate the life that God has given you by focusing your thoughts upon those things that are worthy of praise. Today, count your blessings instead of your hardships. And thank the Giver of all things good for gifts that are simply too numerous to count.

The mind is like a clock that is constantly running down.
It has to be wound up daily with good thoughts.
Fulton J. Sheen

I could go through this day oblivious to the miracles
all around me, or I could tune in and "enjoy."
Gloria Gaither

The things we think are the things that feed our souls.
If we think on pure and lovely things, we shall grow pure
and lovely like them; and the converse is equally true.
Hannah Whitall Smith

I may not be able to change the world I see around me,
but I can change the way I see the world within me.
John Maxwell

Today, create a positive attitude by focusing on opportunities, not roadblocks. Of course you may have experienced disappointments in the past, and you will undoubtedly experience some setbacks in the future. But don't invest large amounts of energy focusing on past misfortunes. Instead, look to the future with optimism and hope.

Who Are You?
You Are a Person Who Trusts God's Timetable

He has made everything appropriate in its time.
He has also put eternity in their hearts, but man cannot discover
the work God has done from beginning to end.

Ecclesiastes 3:11 HCSB

Are you anxious for God to work out His plan for your life? Who isn't? As believers, we all want God to do great things for us and through us, and we want Him to do those things now. But sometimes, God has other plans. Sometimes, God's timetable does not coincide with our own. It's worth noting, however, that God's timetable is always perfect.

The next time you find your patience tested to the limit, remember that the world unfolds according to God's plan, not ours. Sometimes, we must wait patiently, and that's as it should be. After all, think about how patient God has been with us.

Will not the Lord's time be better than your time?

C. H. Spurgeon

God has a designated time when his promise will be fulfilled
and the prayer will be answered.

Jim Cymbala

When there is perplexity there is always guidance—
not always at the moment we ask,
but in good time, which is God's time.
There is no need to fret and stew.

Elisabeth Elliot

Your times are in His hands.
He's in charge of the timetable, so wait patiently.

Kay Arthur

God has very big plans in store for your life, so trust Him and
wait patiently for those plans to unfold. And remember: God's
timing is best, so don't allow yourself to become discouraged if
things don't work out exactly as you wish. Instead of worrying
about your future, entrust it to God.

Who Are You?
You Are a Person Who Is Enthusiastic About Life

*Whatever you do, do it enthusiastically,
as something done for the Lord and not for men.*
Colossians 3:23 HCSB

Do you see each day as a glorious opportunity to serve God and to do His will? Are you enthused about life, or do you struggle through each day giving scarcely a thought to God's blessings? Are you constantly praising God for His gifts, and are you sharing His Good News with the world? And are you excited about the possibilities for service that God has placed before you, whether at home, at work, at church, or at school? You should be.

You are the recipient of Christ's sacrificial love. Accept it enthusiastically and share it fervently. Jesus deserves your enthusiasm; the world deserves it; and you deserve the experience of sharing it.

Catch on fire with enthusiasm and people
will come for miles to watch you burn.

John Wesley

Wherever you are, be all there.
Live to the hilt every situation you believe to be
the will of God.

Jim Elliot

Don't take hold of a thing
unless you want that thing to take hold of you.

E. Stanley Jones

Enthusiasm, like the flu, is contagious—
we get it from one another.

Barbara Johnson

When you become genuinely enthused about your life and
your faith, you'll guard your heart and improve your life.

Who Are You?
You Are a Person Who Is Not Envious

Therefore, laying aside all malice, all deceit, hypocrisy, envy, and all evil speaking, as newborn babes, desire the pure milk of the word, that you may grow thereby.

I Peter 2:1-2 NKJV

Because we are frail, imperfect human beings, we are sometimes envious of others. But God's Word warns us that envy is sin. Thus, we must guard ourselves against the natural tendency to feel resentment and jealousy when other people experience good fortune. As believers, we have absolutely no reason to be envious of any people on earth. After all, as Christians we are already recipients of the greatest gift in all creation: God's grace. We have been promised the gift of eternal life through God's only begotten Son, and we must count that gift as our most precious possession.

So here's a simple suggestion that is guaranteed to bring you happiness: fill your heart with God's love, God's promises, and God's Son . . . and when you do so, leave no room for envy, hatred, bitterness, or regret.

How can you possess the miseries of envy
when you possess in Christ the best of all portions?

C. H. Spurgeon

When you worry about what you don't have,
you won't be able to enjoy what you do have.

Charles Swindoll

What God asks, does, or requires of others is not my
business; it is His.

Kay Arthur

Discontent dries up the soul.

Elisabeth Elliot

Envy is a sin, a sin that robs you of contentment and peace. So
you must steadfastly refuse to let feelings of envy invade your
thoughts or your heart.

Who Are You?
You Are a Person Who Says No to Drugs

Be sober! Be on the alert!
Your adversary the Devil is prowling around like a roaring lion,
looking for anyone he can devour.

1 Peter 5:8 HCSB

D o you hang out with people who consider "partying" to be the most important aspect of their lives? If so, you're headed headlong down a dead-end street . . . right along with your friends.

Mind-altering substances (including the most popular American mind-bender of all: beer) are dangerous . . . make that Dangerous (with a capital D).

So here are three things to remember about alcohol and other drugs: 1. If you're drinking or drugging, you must either stop that behavior or face very disastrous consequences. 2. If you're spending time with people who think that alcohol and drugs are "harmless," you're choosing to associate with some very naïve people. 3. If you're dating someone who drinks or drugs, you deserve better . . . much better. End of lecture.

To many, total abstinence is easier than
perfect moderation.

St. Augustine

Addiction is the most powerful psychic enemy of
humanity's desire for God.

Gerald May

Whatever you love most, be it sports, pleasure,
business or God, that is your god.

Billy Graham

It all starts in the mind and the mouth and springs from
a lack of balance and self-discipline.

Joyce Meyer

Make Jesus your highest priority, and ask Him to help you
overcome any behaviors that might distance you from Him.

Who Are You?
You Are a Person Who Encourages Others

*Let's see how inventive we can be in encouraging love
and helping out, not avoiding worshipping together
as some do but spurring each other on.*

Hebrews 10:24-25 MSG

One of the reasons that God placed you here on earth is so that you might become a beacon of encouragement to the world. As a faithful follower of the One from Galilee, you have every reason to be hopeful, and you have every reason to share your hopes with others. When you do, you will discover that hope, like other human emotions, is contagious.

As a follower of Christ, you are instructed to choose your words carefully so as to build others up through wholesome, honest encouragement (Ephesians 4:29). So look for the good in others and celebrate the good that you find. As the old saying goes, "When someone does something good, applaud—you'll make two people happy."

Encouraging others means helping people,
looking for the best in them,
and trying to bring out their positive qualities.

John Maxwell

As you're rushing through life, take time to stop a moment,
look into people's eyes, say something kind,
and try to make them laugh!

Barbara Johnson

God grant that we may not hinder those who are
battling their way slowly into the light.

Oswald Chambers

I can usually sense that a leading is from the Holy Spirit
when it calls me to humble myself, to serve somebody,
to encourage somebody, or to give something away.
Very rarely will the evil one lead us
to do those kind of things.

Bill Hybels

Sometimes, even a very few words can make a very big difference. As Fanny Crosby observed, "A single word, if spoken in a friendly spirit, may be sufficient to turn one from dangerous error."

Who Are You?
You Are a Person Who Walks in the Light

Then Jesus spoke to them again:
"I am the light of the world. Anyone who follows Me will never
walk in the darkness, but will have the light of life."
John 8:12 HCSB

God's Holy Word instructs us that Jesus is, "the way, the truth, and the life" (John 14:6-7). Without Christ, we are as far removed from salvation as the east is removed from the west. And without Christ, we can never know the ultimate truth: God's truth.

Truth is God's way: He commands His believers to live in truth, and He rewards those who do so. Jesus is the personification of God's liberating truth, a truth that offers salvation to mankind.

Do you seek to walk with God? Do you seek to feel His presence and His peace? Then you must walk in truth; you must walk in the light; you must walk with the Savior. There is simply no other way.

Victory is the result of Christ's life lived out in the believer.
It is important to see that victory, not defeat,
is God's purpose for His children.

Corrie ten Boom

Jesus differs from all other teachers; they reach the ear,
but he instructs the heart; they deal with the outward letter,
but he imparts an inward taste for the truth.

C. H. Spurgeon

It's your heart that Jesus longs for:
your will to be made His own with self on the cross forever,
and Jesus alone on the throne.

Ruth Bell Graham

In the dark? Follow the Son.

Anonymous

Nobody can find Him for you. God is searching for you; it's up
to you—and you alone—to open your heart to Him.

Who Are You?
You Are a Person Who
Strives to Live Righteously

*And we pray this in order that you may live a life worthy of
the Lord and may please him in every way:
bearing fruit in every good work,
growing in the knowledge of God.*

Colossians 1:10 NIV

When we behave ourselves as thoughtful Christians—and when we conduct ourselves in accordance with God's instructions—we are blessed in ways that we cannot fully understand. When we seek righteousness in our own lives—and when we seek the companionship of those who do likewise—we reap the spiritual rewards that God intends for us to enjoy.

Today, as you fulfill your responsibilities, hold fast to that which is good, and associate yourself with folks who behave themselves in like fashion. When you do, your good works will serve as a powerful example for others and as a worthy offering to your Creator. And you will reap a surprising array of blessings as a result of your good works.

We are to leave an impression on all those we meet
that communicates whose we are
and what kingdom we represent.

Lisa Bevere

Never support an experience which does not have God
as its source and faith in God as its result.

Oswald Chambers

The best evidence of our having the truth is
our walking in the truth.

Matthew Henry

I don't care what a man says he believes with his lips.
I want to know with a vengeance what he says
with his life and his actions.

Sam Jones

Because God is just, He rewards good behavior just as surely
as He punishes sin. And there aren't any loopholes.

Who Are You?
You Are a Person Who Is
Kind to Everybody

And be kind and compassionate to one another,
forgiving one another,
just as God also forgave you in Christ.
Ephesians 4:32 HCSB

Would you like an ironclad formula for improved self-esteem? Try this: be kind to everybody.

Kindness is a choice. Sometimes, when you feel happy or generous, you may find it easy to be kind. Other times, when you are discouraged or tired, you can scarcely summon the energy to utter a single kind word. But, God's commandment is clear: He intends that you make the conscious choice to treat others with kindness and respect, no matter your circumstances, no matter your emotions.

So today, spread a heaping helping of kindness wherever you go. When you do, you'll discover that the more kindness you give away to others, the more you'll receive in return.

A little kindly advice is better than
a great deal of scolding.

Fanny Crosby

When you launch an act of kindness out into
the crosswinds of life, it will blow kindness back to you.

Dennis Swanberg

When you extend hospitality to others,
you're not trying to impress people,
you're trying to reflect God to them.

Max Lucado

Do all the good you can. By all the means you can.
In all the ways you can. In all the places you can.
At all the times you can. To all the people you can.
As long as ever you can.

John Wesley

The Golden Rule starts with you, so when in doubt, be a little kinder than necessary. You'll feel better about yourself when you do.

Who Are You?
You Are a Person Who Keeps Learning

It takes knowledge to fill a home
with rare and beautiful treasures.
Proverbs 24:4 NCV

Another way to feel better about yourself is to keep acquiring both knowledge and wisdom. Knowledge is found in textbooks. Wisdom, on the other hand, is found in God's Holy Word and in the carefully-chosen words of loving parents, family members, and friends.

Knowledge is an important building block in a well-lived life, and it pays rich dividends both personally and professionally. But, wisdom is even more important because it refashions not only the mind, but also the heart.

When you study God's Word and live according to His commandments, you will become wise . . . and you will be a blessing to your family and to the world.

While chastening is always difficult, if we look to God
for the lesson we should learn, we will see spiritual fruit.

Vonette Bright

The wonderful thing about God's schoolroom is that
we get to grade our own papers. You see, He doesn't test us
so He can learn how well we're doing.
He tests us so we can discover how well we're doing.

Charles Swindoll

The wise man gives proper appreciation in his life
to his past. He learns to sift the sawdust of heritage
in order to find the nuggets that make
the current moment have any meaning.

Grady Nutt

It's the things you learn after you know it all
that really count.

Vance Havner

Keep learning. The future belongs to those who are willing to
do the work that's required to prepare for it.

Who Are You?
You Are a Person Who
Avoids the Media Hype

No one should deceive himself. If anyone among you thinks he is wise in this age, he must become foolish so that he can become wise. For the wisdom of this world is foolishness with God, since it is written: He catches the wise in their craftiness.

I Corinthians 3:18-19 HCSB

Sometimes it's hard being a Christian, especially when the world keeps pumping out messages that are contrary to your faith.

The media is working around the clock in an attempt to rearrange your priorities. The media says that your appearance is all-important, that your clothes are all-important, that your car is all-important, and that partying is all-important. But guess what? Those messages are lies. The important things in your life have little to do with parties or appearances. The all-important things in life have to do with your faith, your family, and your future. Period.

Are you willing to stand up for your faith? If so, you'll be doing yourself a king-sized favor. And consider this: When you begin to speak up for God, isn't it logical to assume that you'll also begin to know Him in a more meaningful way? Of course you will.

So do yourself a favor: forget the media hype, and pay attention to God. Stand up for Him and be counted, not just in church where it's relatively easy to be a Christian, but also outside the church, where it's significantly harder. You owe it God . . . and you owe it to yourself.

I have a divided heart, trying to love God and the world at the same time. God says, "You can't love me as you should if you love this world too."

Mary Morrison Suggs

The only ultimate disaster that can befall us, I have come to realize, is to feel ourselves to be home on earth.

Max Lucado

The media is sending out messages that are dangerous to your physical, emotional, and spiritual health. If you choose to believe those messages, you're setting yourself up for lots of trouble.

Who Are You?
You Are a Person Who Can Say No

Discretion will protect you
and understanding will guard you.
Proverbs 2:11 NIV

When your peers encourage you to do things that you know are wrong, do you have enough confidence to say no? Hopefully so. But if you haven't quite learned the art of saying no, don't feel like the Lone Ranger—plenty of people much older than you still have trouble standing up for themselves.

An important part of growing up is learning how to assert yourself. Another part of growing up is learning when to say no. For most people, these are lessons that take a long time to learn, so if you're wise, you'll start learning them sooner rather than later. Remember: you have the right to say no, and you have the right to say it right now!

Choose the opposition of the whole world
rather than offend Jesus.

Thomas à Kempis

A thoughtful Christian doesn't follow the crowd
unless the crowd is following Jesus.

Anonymous

For better or worse, you will eventually become more
and more like the people you associate with.
So why not associate with people
who make you better, not worse?

Marie T. Freeman

True friends will always lift you higher and challenge you
to walk in a manner pleasing to our Lord.

Lisa Bevere

Slow Down! If you're about to make an important decision,
don't be impulsive. Remember: big decisions have big consequences, and if you don't think about those consequences
now, you may pay a big price later.

Who Are You?
You Are a Person Who Thinks Optimistically About Yourself and Your Life

But if we hope for what we do not see,
we eagerly wait for it with patience.
Romans 8:25 HCSB

Are you an optimist or a pessimist? The answer to this question will determine, to a surprising extent, how you feel about yourself.

As you look at the landscape of your life, do you see opportunities, possibilities, and blessings, or do you focus, instead, upon the more negative scenery? Do you spend more time counting your blessings or your misfortunes? If you've acquired the unfortunate habit of focusing too intently upon the negative aspects of your life, then your spiritual vision is in need of correction.

The way that you choose to view the scenery around you will have a profound impact on the quality, the tone, and the direction of your life. The more you focus on the beauty that surrounds you, the more beautiful your own life becomes.

Christ can put a spring in your step
and a thrill in your heart. Optimism and cheerfulness are
products of knowing Christ.

Billy Graham

It is a remarkable thing that some of the most optimistic
and enthusiastic people you will meet are those
who have been through intense suffering.

Warren Wiersbe

The Christian lifestyle is not one of legalistic do's and don'ts,
but one that is positive, attractive, and joyful.

Vonette Bright

Developing a positive attitude means working continually
to find what is uplifting and encouraging.

Barbara Johnson

If you think you can do something, you probably can. If you
think you can't do something, you probably can't. That's why
it's so important to believe in yourself.

Who Are You?
You Are a Person Who Knows
When Not to Quit

So we must not get tired of doing good,
for we will reap at the proper time if we don't give up.
Galatians 6:9 HCSB

The occasional disappointments and failures of life are inevitable. Such setbacks are simply the price that we must pay for our willingness to take risks as we follow our dreams. But even when we encounter setbacks, we must never lose faith.

The reassuring words of Hebrews 10:36 serve as a comforting reminder that perseverance indeed pays: "You have need of endurance, so that when you have done the will of God, you may receive what was promised" (NASB).

Are you willing to trust God's Word? And are you willing to keep "fighting the good fight," even when you've experienced unexpected difficulties? If so, you may soon be surprised at the creative ways that God finds to help determined people like you . . . people who possess the wisdom and the courage to persevere.

Failure is one of life's most powerful teachers.
How we handle our failures determines whether
we're going to simply "get by" in life or "press on."

Beth Moore

Every achievement worth remembering is stained
with the blood of diligence and scarred by
the wounds of disappointment.

Charles Swindoll

Keep adding, keep walking, keep advancing; do not stop,
do not turn back, do not turn from the straight road.

St. Augustine

By perseverance the snail reached the ark.

C. H. Spurgeon

If things don't work out at first, don't quit. If you never try,
you'll never know how good you can be.

Who Are You?
You Are a Person Who
Prays Early and Often

Be cheerful no matter what; pray all the time;
thank God no matter what happens. This is the way God
wants you who belong to Christ Jesus to live.

1 Thessalonians 5:16-18 MSG

Perhaps, because of your demanding schedule, you've neglected to pay sufficient attention to a particularly important part of your life: the spiritual part. If so, today is the day to change, and one way to make that change is simply to spend a little more time talking with God.

God is trying to get His message through to you. Are you listening?

Perhaps, on occasion, you may find yourself overwhelmed by the press of everyday life. Perhaps you may forget to slow yourself down long enough to talk with God. Instead of turning your thoughts and prayers to Him, you may rely upon our own resources. Instead of asking God for guidance, you may depend only upon your own limited wisdom. A far better course of action is this: simply stop what you're doing long enough to open your heart to God; then listen carefully for His directions.

In all things great and small, seek God's wisdom and His grace. He hears your prayers, and He will answer. All you must do is ask.

Four things let us ever keep in mind: God hears prayer,
God heeds payer, God answers prayer,
and God delivers by prayer.
E. M. Bounds

We must pray literally without ceasing, in every occurrence
and employment of our lives. You know I mean that prayer of
the heart which is independent of place or situation,
or which is, rather, a habit of lifting up the heart to God,
as in a constant communication with Him.
Elizabeth Ann Seton

Do nothing at all unless you begin with prayer.
Ephraem the Syrian

Of course you should pray at mealtime and bedtime, but that's just the beginning. You can offer lots of prayers to God all day long . . . and you should!

Who Are You?
You Are a Person Who Says No to Immorality

Therefore, brothers, by the mercies of God,
I urge you to present your bodies as a living sacrifice,
holy and pleasing to God; this is your spiritual worship.
Romans 12:1 HCSB

The decision to have sex before you're married—or the decision to abstain from it—is a choice that will most certainly impact the rest of your life. That decision will play an important role in the way you see yourself, and it will play an important role in the way you view relationships with members of the opposite sex. And of course, there's always the chance that your decision to have sex might result in an unexpected "surprise."

Face it: there's a lot riding on the decision to abstain from sex. And because it's an important decision, you should think about it—and pray about it—before you make a decision that might just change the direction of your life.

As you're making up your mind about the role that sex will play in your life, trust the quiet inner voice of your conscience, and be obedient to the teaching you find in God's Word. When you do, you'll make the right decision . . . and you'll be eternally grateful that you did.

A pure theology and a loose morality will never mix.
C. H. Spurgeon

A life lived in God is not lived on the plane of feelings,
but of the will.
Elisabeth Elliot

Morality and immorality are not defined by man's changing
attitudes and social customs. They are determined by
the God of the universe, whose timeless standards
cannot be ignored with impunity.
James Dobson

When we do what is right, we have contentment,
peace, and happiness.
Beverly LaHaye

If you are a Christian, your hero (and the One you should seek
to imitate) is Christ. So follow in His footsteps and obey His
commandments. When you do, you'll be secure.

Who Are You?
You Are a Person Who Knows
How to Listen

The one who is from God listens to God's words.
This is why you don't listen, because you are not from God.
John 8:47 HCSB

Sometimes God speaks loudly and clearly. More often, He speaks in a quiet voice—and if you are wise, you will be listening carefully when He does. To do so, you must carve out quiet moments each day to study His Word and sense His direction.

Can you quiet yourself long enough to listen to your conscience? Are you attuned to the subtle guidance of your intuition? Are you willing to pray sincerely and then to wait quietly for God's response? Hopefully so. Usually God refrains from sending His messages on stone tablets or city billboards. More often, He communicates in subtler ways. If you sincerely desire to hear His voice, you must listen carefully, and you must do so in the silent corners of your quiet, willing heart.

Listening is loving.
Zig Ziglar

In the soul-searching of our lives,
we are to stay quiet so we can hear Him say all that
He wants to say to us in our hearts.
Charles Swindoll

When we come to Jesus stripped of pretensions,
with a needy spirit, ready to listen,
He meets us at the point of need.
Catherine Marshall

God is always listening.
Stormie Omartian

Prayer is two-way communication with God. Talking to God
isn't enough; you should also listen to Him.

Who Are You?
You Are a Person Who Understands the Need for Balance

Grow a wise heart—you'll do yourself a favor;
keep a clear head—you'll find a good life.
Proverbs 19:8 MSG

Face facts: life is a delicate balancing act, a tightrope walk with over-commitment on one side and under-commitment on the other. And it's up to each of us to walk carefully on that rope, not falling prey to pride (which causes us to attempt too much) or to fear (which causes us to attempt too little).

God's Word promises us the possibility of abundance (John 10:10). And we are far more likely to experience that abundance when we lead balanced lives.

Are you doing too much—or too little? If so, it's time to have a little chat with God. And if you listen carefully to His instructions, you will strive to achieve a more balanced life, a life that's right for you and your loved ones. When you do, everybody wins.

We are all created differently. We share a common need
to balance the different parts of our lives.

Dr. Walt Larimore

Always remember that we can learn to control our
weaknesses through the power of the Holy Spirit
and in doing so become well-balanced individuals who
cannot be controlled by Satan.

Joyce Meyer

Does God care about all the responsibilities we have to
juggle in our daily lives? Of course. But he cares more that
our lives demonstrate balance, the ability to discern
what is essential and give ourselves fully to it.

Penelope Stokes

Strive for balance. Lots of people are clamoring for your
attention, your time, and your energy. It's up to you to
establish priorities that are important for you and your family.
And remember, if you don't establish priorities, the world has
a way of doing the job for you.

Who Are You?
You Are a Person Who
Chooses to Please God

Do you think I am trying to make people accept me?
No, God is the One I am trying to please.
Am I trying to please people? If I still wanted to please people,
I would not be a servant of Christ.

Galatians 1:10 NCV

Sometimes, it's very tempting to be a people-pleaser. But usually, it's the wrong thing to do.

When you worry too much about pleasing dates or friends, you may not worry enough about pleasing God—and when you fail to please God, you inevitably pay a very high price for our mistaken priorities.

Whom will you try to please today: God or your friends? Your obligation is most certainly not to your peers or to your date. Your obligation is to an all-knowing and perfect God. Trust Him always. Love Him always. Praise Him always. And seek to please Him and only Him. Always.

People who constantly, and fervently,
seek the approval of others live with an identity crisis.
They don't know who they are, and they are defined by
what others think of them.

Charles Stanley

God is not hard to please. He does not expect us to be
absolutely perfect. He just expects us to keep moving toward
Him and believing in Him, letting Him work with us
to bring us into conformity to His will and ways.

Joyce Meyer

Every day, I find countless opportunities to decide
whether I will obey God and demonstrate my love for Him
or try to please myself or the world system.
God is waiting for my choices.

Bill Bright

If you are burdened with a "people-pleasing" personality,
outgrow it. Realize that you can't please all of the people all of
the time (including your dates), nor should you attempt to.

Who Are You?
You Are a Person Who Understands and Resists Evil

*Take your stand with God's loyal community and live,
or chase after phantoms of evil and die.*
Proverbs 11:19 MSG

The better you get to know God, the more you'll understand how God wants you to respond to evil. And make no mistake, this world is inhabited by quite a few people who are very determined to do evil things. The devil and his human helpers are working 24/7 to cause pain and heartbreak in every corner of the globe . . . including your corner. So you'd better beware.

Your job, if you choose to accept it, is to recognize evil and fight it. The moment that you decide to fight evil whenever you see it, you can no longer be a lukewarm, halfhearted Christian. And, when you are no longer a lukewarm Christian, God rejoices while the devil despairs.

When will you choose to get serious about fighting the evils of our world? Before you answer that question, consider this: in the battle of good versus evil, the devil never takes a day off . . . and neither should you.

Rebuke the Enemy in your own name and he laughs;
command him in the name of Christ and he flees.

John Eldredge

Of two evils, choose neither.

C. H. Spurgeon

He who passively accepts evil is as much involved in it as
he who helps to perpetrate it. He who accepts evil without
protesting against it is really cooperating with it.

Martin Luther King, Jr.

God loves you, and He yearns for you to turn away from
the path of evil. You need His forgiveness, and you need Him
to come into your life and remake you from within.

Billy Graham

Evil does exist, and you will confront it. Prepare yourself by
forming a genuine, life-changing relationship with God and His
only begotten Son. There is darkness in this world, but God's
light can overpower any darkness.

Who Are You?
You Are a Person Who
Trusts God's Wisdom

*Understanding is like a fountain which gives
life to those who use it.*

Proverbs 16:22 NCV

The world has its own brand of wisdom, a brand of wisdom that is often wrong and sometimes dangerous. God, on the other hand, has a different brand of wisdom, a wisdom that will lead you closer to Him.

Where will you place your trust today? Will you trust in the wisdom of fallible men and women, or will you place your faith in God's perfect wisdom? The answer to this question will determine the direction of your day and the quality of your decisions.

Are you tired? Discouraged? Fearful? Be comforted and trust God. Are you worried or anxious? Be confident in God's power. Are you confused? Listen to the quiet voice of your Heavenly Father—He is not a God of confusion. Talk with Him; listen to Him; trust Him. His wisdom, unlike the "wisdom" of the world, will never let you down.

God does not give His counsel to the curious
or the careless; He reveals His will to the concerned
and to the consecrated.

Warren Wiersbe

The center of power is not to be found in summit meetings
or in peace conferences. It is not in Peking or Washington
or the United Nations, but rather where a child of God prays
in the power of the Spirit for God's will to be done in her life,
in her home, and in the world around her.

Ruth Bell Graham

Most of us go through life praying a little, planning a little,
jockeying for position, hoping but never being quite certain
of anything, and always secretly afraid that we will miss the
way. This is a tragic waste of truth and never gives rest to
the heart. There is a better way. It is to repudiate our own
wisdom and take instead the infinite wisdom of God.

A. W. Tozer

God's wisdom is perfect, and it's available to you. So if you
want to become wise, become a student of God's Word and a
follower of His Son.

Who Are You?
You Are a Person Who Lives
by the Golden Rule

Just as you want others to do for you, do the same for them.
Luke 6:31 HCSB

Jesus made Himself perfectly clear: He instructed you to treat other people in the same way that you want to be treated. But sometimes, especially when you're feeling pressure from friends, or when you're tired or upset, obeying the Golden Rule can seem like an impossible task—but it's not.

God wants each of us to treat other people with respect, kindness, and courtesy. He wants us to rise above our own imperfections, and He wants us to treat others with unselfishness and love. To make it short and sweet, God wants us to obey the Golden Rule, and He knows we can do it.

So if you're wondering how to treat someone else, ask the person you see every time you look into the mirror. The answer you receive will tell you exactly what to do.

Faith never asks whether good works are to be done,
but has done them before there is time to ask
the question, and it is always doing them.
Martin Luther

When you extend hospitality to others,
you're not trying to impress people,
you're trying to reflect God to them.
Max Lucado

If we have the true love of God in our hearts,
we will show it in our lives. We will not have to
go up and down the earth proclaiming it.
We will show it in everything we say or do.
D. L. Moody

The Golden Rule starts at home,
but it should never stop there.
Marie T. Freeman

Someone very near you may need a helping hand or a kind word, so keep your eyes open, and look for people who need your help, whether at home, at church, or at school.

Who Are You?
You Are a Person Who Avoids Gossip

So rid yourselves of all wickedness, all deceit,
hypocrisy, envy, and all slander.
I Peter 2:1 HCSB

Face facts: gossip is the guilty little pleasure that tempts almost all of us from time to time. Why is it so tempting to gossip? Because when we put other people down, we experience a brief dose of self-righteousness as we look down our noses at the misdeeds of others. But there's a catch: in truth, we can never really build ourselves up by tearing other people down. So the habit of gossip turns out to be a self-defeating waste of time.

It's no wonder that the Bible clearly teaches that gossip is wrong. Consider the simple advice found in Proverbs 16:28, "Gossip ruins friendships" (NCV). So do yourself a big favor: don't spend precious time talking about other people. It's a waste of words, it's the wrong thing to do, and in the end, it will leave you with less self-respect, not more.

When you avoid the temptation to engage in gossip, you'll feel better about yourself—and other people will feel better about you, too. So don't do it.

I still believe we ought to talk about Jesus.
The old country doctor of my boyhood days always began
his examination by saying, "Let me see your tongue."
That's a good way to check a Christian: the tongue test.
Let's hear what he is talking about.

Vance Havner

Would we want our hidden sins to be divulged?
Then we should be silent about the hidden sins of others.

St. Jean Baptiste de la Salle

To belittle is to be little.

Anonymous

We should have great peace if we did not busy ourselves
with what others say and do.

Thomas à Kempis

When talking about other people, use this guideline: don't say
something behind someone's back that you wouldn't say to
that person directly.

Who Are You?
You Are a Person Who
Guards Your Heart and Mind

*Summing it all up, friends, I'd say you'll do best by filling
your minds and meditating on things true, noble, reputable,
authentic, compelling, gracious, the best, not the worst;
the beautiful, not the ugly; things to praise, not things to curse.
Put into practice what you learned from me, what you heard
and saw and realized. Do that, and God,
who makes everything work together, will work you
into his most excellent harmonies.*

Philippians 4:8-9 MSG

You are near and dear to God. He loves you more than you can imagine, and He wants the very best for you. And one more thing: God wants you to guard your heart.

Every day, you are faced with choices . . . lots of them. You can do the right thing, or not. You can tell the truth, or not. You can be kind, generous, and obedient. Or not.

Today, the world will offer you countless opportunities to let down your guard and, by doing so, let the devil do his worst. So be watchful and obedient. Guard your heart by giving it to your Heavenly Father; it is safe with Him.

Do nothing that you would not like to be doing when Jesus comes. Go no place where you would not like to be found when He returns.

Corrie ten Boom

The man who only shuns temptations outwardly and does not uproot them inwardly will make little progress; indeed the sins will quickly return, more violent than before.

Thomas à Kempis

Prayer guards hearts and minds and causes God to bring peace out of chaos.

Beth Moore

Prayer is our pathway not only to divine protection, but also to a personal, intimate relationship with God.

Shirley Dobson

If you're not sure what to do . . . slow down and listen to your conscience. That little voice inside your head is remarkably dependable, but you can't depend upon it if you never listen to it. So stop, listen, and learn—your conscience is almost always right!

Who Are You?
You Are a Person Who Forms Habits That Are Pleasing to God

*I, the Lord, examine the mind,
I test the heart to give to each according to his way,
according to what his actions deserve.*
Jeremiah 17:10 HCSB

It's an old saying and a true one: First, you make your habits, and then your habits make you. Some habits will inevitably bring you closer to God; other habits will lead you away from the path He has chosen for you. If you sincerely desire to improve your spiritual health, you must honestly examine the habits that make up the fabric of your day. And you must abandon those habits that are displeasing to God.

If you trust God, and if you keep asking for His help, He can transform your life. If you sincerely ask Him to help you, the same God who created the universe will help you defeat the harmful habits that have heretofore defeated you. So, if at first you don't succeed, keep praying. God is listening, and He's ready to help you become a better person if you ask Him . . . so ask today.

You can build up a set of good habits so that you habitually take the Christian way without thought.

E. Stanley Jones

You will never change your life until you change something you do daily.

John Maxwell

If you want to form a new habit, get to work. If you want to break a bad habit, get on your knees.

Marie T. Freeman

Since behaviors become habits, make them work with you and not against you.

E. Stanley Jones

First you make your habits; then your habits make you. So it's always a good time to think about the kind of person your habits are making you.

Who Are You?
You Are a Person Who Makes Up
Your Mind to Be Happy

Rejoice in the Lord always. I will say it again: Rejoice!
Philippians 4:4 HCSB

Happiness depends less upon our circumstances than upon our thoughts. When we turn our thoughts to God, to His gifts, and to His glorious creation, we experience the joy that God intends for His children. But, when we focus on the negative aspects of life, we inadvertently bring needless pain to our friends, to our families, and to ourselves.

Do you sincerely want to be a happy person? Then set your mind and your heart upon God's love and His grace. Seek a genuine, intimate, life-altering relationship with your Creator by studying His Word and trusting His promises. And while you're at it, count your blessings instead of your hardships. Then, after you've done these things, claim the joy, the peace, and the spiritual abundance that the Shepherd offers His sheep.

Men spend their lives in anticipation, in determining
to be vastly happy at some period or other,
when they have time. But the present time has one
advantage over every other: it is ours.

Charles Caleb Colton

Life is 10% what happens to you
and 90% how you respond to it.

Charles Swindoll

It's your choice: you can either count your blessings
or recount your disappointments.

Jim Gallery

We will never be happy until we make God the source of
our fulfillment and the answer to our longings.

Stormie Omartian

If you want to find lasting happiness, don't chase it. Instead,
do your duty, obey your God, and wait for happiness to find
you.

Who Are You?
You Are a Person Who Chooses to Answer the Call

God chose you to be his people,
so I urge you now to live the life to which God called you.
Ephesians 4:1 NCV

If you really want to figure out who you are—and who you should become—it is vitally important that you heed God's call. In John 15:16, Jesus says, "You did not choose me, but I chose you and appointed you to go and bear fruit—fruit that will last" (NIV). In other words, you have been called by Christ, and now, it is up to you to decide precisely how you will answer.

Have you already found your special calling? If so, you're a very lucky person. If not, keep searching and keep praying until you discover it. And remember this: God has important work for you to do—work that no one else on earth can accomplish but you.

When you become consumed by God's call on your life, everything will take on new meaning and significance. You will begin to see every facet of your life, including your pain, as a means through which God can work to bring others to Himself.

Charles Stanley

Whatever purpose motivates your life, it must be something big enough and grand enough to make the investment worthwhile.

Warren Wiersbe

God wants to revolutionize our lives—by showing us how knowing Him can be the most powerful force to help us become all we want to be.

Bill Hybels

God has a plan for your life, a divine calling that you can either answer or ignore. How you choose to respond to God's calling will determine the direction you take and the contributions you make.

Who Are You?
You Are a Person Who Entrusts Your Hopes to God

*You, Lord, give true peace to those who depend on you,
because they trust you.*

Isaiah 26:3 NCV

Have you ever felt hope for the future slipping away? If so, you have temporarily lost sight of the hope that we, as believers, must place in the promises of our Heavenly Father. If you are feeling discouraged, worried, or worse, remember the words of Psalm 31:24: "Be of good courage, and He shall strengthen your heart, all you who hope in the Lord" (NKJV).

Of course, we will face disappointments and failures, but these are only temporary defeats. Of course, this world can be a place of trials and tribulations, but we are secure. God has promised us peace, joy, and eternal life. And God keeps His promises today, tomorrow, and forever.

Hope is faith holding out its hand in the dark.

Barbara Johnson

The will of God is the most delicious
and delightful thing in the universe.

Hannah Whitall Smith

It is more serious to lose hope than to sin.

John of Carpathos

God's purposes are often hidden from us.
He owes us no explanations.
We owe Him our complete love and trust.

Warren Wiersbe

Don't give up hope: Other people have experienced the same
kind of hard times you may be experiencing now. They made
it, and so can you. (Psalm 146:5)

Who Are You?
You Are a Person Who Values Integrity

A good name is to be chosen over great wealth.
Proverbs 22:1 HCSB

Hey, would you like a time-tested, ironclad formula for success? Here it is: guard your integrity like you guard your wallet.

It has been said on many occasions and in many ways that honesty is the best policy. For Christians, it is far more important to note that honesty is God's policy. And if we are to be servants worthy of our Savior, Jesus Christ, we must be honest, forthright, and trustworthy.

Telling the truth means telling the whole truth. And that means summoning the courage to deliver bad news when necessary. And for some of us, especially those of us who are card-carrying people pleasers, telling the whole truth can be difficult indeed (especially if we're pretty sure that the truth will make somebody mad). Still, if we wish to fashion successful lives, we've got to learn to be totally truthful—part-time truth-telling doesn't cut the mustard.

Sometimes, honesty is difficult; sometimes, honesty is painful; sometimes, honesty is inconvenient; but honesty is always God's way. In the Book of Proverbs, we read, "The Lord detests lying lips, but he delights in men who are truthful" (12:22 NIV). Clearly, truth is God's way, and it must be our way, too, even when telling the truth is difficult.

God never called us to naïveté. He called us to integrity....
The biblical concept of integrity emphasizes mature
innocence not childlike ignorance.
Beth Moore

Integrity is the glue that holds our way of life together.
We must constantly strive to keep our integrity intact.
When wealth is lost, nothing is lost; when health is lost,
something is lost; when character is lost, all is lost.
Billy Graham

Our life pursuits will reflect our character
and personal integrity.
Franklin Graham

Take time to think about ways that you can remove yourself from situations that might compromise your integrity.

Who Are You?
You Are a Person Who Is
a Worthy Disciple

He has told you men what is good and what it is the Lord
requires of you: Only to act justly, to love faithfulness,
and to walk humbly with your God.

Micah 6:8 HCSB

When Jesus addressed His disciples, He warned that each one must, "take up his cross and follow Me." The disciples must have known exactly what the Master meant. In Jesus' day, prisoners were forced to carry their own crosses to the location where they would be put to death. Thus, Christ's message was clear: in order to follow Him, Christ's disciples must deny themselves and, instead, trust Him completely. Nothing has changed since then.

If we are to be disciples of Christ, we must trust Him and place Him at the very center of our beings. Jesus never comes "next." He is always first.

Do you seek to be a worthy disciple of Christ? Then pick up His cross today and every day that you live. When you do, He will bless you now and forever.

Discipleship is a daily discipline:
we follow Jesus a step at a time, a day at a time.
Warren Wiersbe

Discipleship means personal, passionate devotion
to a Person, our Lord Jesus Christ.
Oswald Chambers

Discipleship is a decision to live by
what I know about God, not by what I feel
about him or myself or my neighbors.
Eugene Peterson

Discipleship means allegiance to the suffering Christ,
and it is therefore not at all surprising that
Christians should be called upon to suffer.
Dietrich Bonhoeffer

Jesus has invited you to become His disciple. If you accept His invitation—and if you obey His commandments—you will be protected and blessed.

Who Are You?
You Are a Person Who Pays Attention to What's Happening Around You

*Pay careful attention, then, to how you walk—
not as unwise people but as wise.*
Ephesians 5:15 HCSB

You can learn a lot about life, love, and the pursuit of happiness by paying attention to the things that happen around you—so keep your eyes and ears open. And while you're at it, please try to remember that "denial" isn't a big river in Egypt (it is, in truth, the natural human tendency to ignore little problems until they grow too big to ignore).

God is trying to teach you things, and you can learn these lessons the easy way (by paying attention, by learning from other people's mistakes, and by obeying God's commandments) or the hard way (by making your own mistakes, and by continuing to make them over and over again until you finally learn something). Of course, it's better to learn things sooner rather than later . . . starting now. So what are you waiting for?

Experience has taught me that the Shepherd is
far more willing to show His sheep the path than
the sheep are to follow. He is endlessly merciful,
patient, tender, and loving. If we, His stupid and
wayward sheep, really want to be led,
we will without fail be led. Of that I am sure.

Elisabeth Elliot

Believe and do what God says.
The life-changing consequences will be limitless,
and the results will be confidence and peace of mind.

Franklin Graham

Much guilt arises in the life of the believer from practicing
the chameleon life of environmental adaptation.

Beth Moore

Do you find yourself in the same kind of trouble over and over again? If so, there's something in your life that needs to be fixed—and you've probably been trying to ignore it. Ignore no more! You'll never fix the problems that you're unwilling to acknowledge.

Who Are You?
You Are a Person Who Turns to God for Strength

God is our refuge and strength,
a helper who is always found in times of trouble.
Psalm 46:1 HCSB

All of us face difficult days. Sometimes even the most devout Christians can become discouraged, and you are no exception. After all, you live in a world where expectations can be high and demands can be even higher.

If you find yourself enduring difficult circumstances, remember that God remains in His heaven. If you become discouraged with the direction of your day or your life, turn your thoughts and prayers to Him. He is a God of possibility, not negativity. He will guide you through your difficulties and beyond them. And then, with a renewed spirit of optimism and hope, you can thank the Giver of all things good for gifts that are simply too numerous to count.

Even in the winter, even in the midst of the storm,
the sun is still there. Somewhere, up above the clouds,
it still shines and warms and pulls at the life buried
deep inside the brown branches and frozen earth.
The sun is there! Spring will come.

Gloria Gaither

When life is difficult, God wants us to have
a faith that trusts and waits.

Kay Arthur

The strengthening of faith comes from staying with it in
the hour of trial. We should not shrink from tests of faith.

Catherine Marshall

Our heavenly Father never takes anything from his children
unless he means to give them something better.

George Mueller

In dealing with difficult situations, view God as your comfort
and your strength. And remember: Tough times can also be
times of intense personal growth.

Who Are You?
You Are a Person Who Understands the Need to Be Disciplined

But I discipline my body and bring it into subjection,
lest, when I have preached to others,
I myself should become disqualified.
I Corinthians 9:27 NKJV

Are you a self-disciplined person? If so, congratulations . . . your disciplined approach to life can help you build a more meaningful relationship with God. Why? Because God expects all His believers (including you) to lead lives of disciplined obedience to Him . . . and He rewards those believers who do.

God doesn't reward laziness, misbehavior, or apathy. God is less concerned with your party time than He is with your prayer time. And God wants all His followers (including you) to behave with dignity and self-control.

So if you want to know God more intimately, try becoming a more disciplined person. When you do, you'll be rewarded—richly rewarded—for your efforts.

Simply stated, self-discipline is obedience to God's Word
and willingness to submit everything in life
to His will, for His ultimate glory.

John MacArthur

As we seek to become disciples of Jesus Christ,
we should never forget that the word *disciple* is directly
related to the word *discipline*. To be a disciple of the Lord
Jesus Christ is to know his discipline.

Dennis Swanberg

Personal humility is a spiritual discipline
and the hallmark of the service of Jesus.

Franklin Graham

If one examines the secret behind a championship football
team, a magnificent orchestra, or a successful business,
the principal ingredient is invariably discipline.

James Dobson

If you find yourself hanging out with undisciplined kids who
are trying to make their world a non-stop party, change friends
. . . fast.

Who Are You?
You Are a Person Who Looks Past All Those Distractions

Look straight ahead, and fix your eyes on what lies before you.
Mark out a straight path for your feet;
then stick to the path and stay safe. Don't get sidetracked;
keep your feet from following evil.
Proverbs 4:25-27 NLT

All of us must live through those days when the traffic jams, the computer crashes, and the dog makes a main course out of our homework. But, when we find ourselves distracted by the minor frustrations of life, we must catch ourselves, take a deep breath, and lift our thoughts upward.

Although we may, at times, struggle mightily to rise above the distractions of everyday living, we need never struggle alone. God is here—eternal and faithful, with infinite patience and love—and, if we reach out to Him, He will restore our sense of perspective and give peace to our souls.

Paul did one thing. Most of us dabble in forty things.
Are you a doer or a dabbler?

Vance Havner

As long as Jesus is one of many options, he is no option.

Max Lucado

When Jesus is in our midst, He brings His limitless power
along as well. But, Jesus must be in the middle,
all eyes and hearts focused on Him.

Shirley Dobson

We need to stop focusing on our lacks and stop giving out
excuses and start looking at and listening to Jesus.

Anne Graham Lotz

With all the distractions in the world, let Jesus be your main
attraction.

Who Are You?
You Are a Person with Big Dreams

Live full lives, full in the fullness of God. God can do anything,
you know—far more than you could ever imagine or guess
or request in your wildest dreams! He does it not by
pushing us around but by working within us,
his Spirit deeply and gently within us.
Ephesians 3:19-20 MSG

Are you willing to entertain the possibility that God has big plans in store for you? Hopefully so. Yet sometimes, especially if you've recently experienced a life-altering disappointment, you may find it difficult to envision a brighter future for yourself and your family. If so, it's time to reconsider your own capabilities . . . and God's.

Your Heavenly Father created you with unique gifts and untapped talents; your job is to tap them. When you do, you'll begin to feel an increasing sense of confidence in yourself and in your future.

It takes courage to dream big dreams. You will discover that courage when you do three things: accept the past, trust God to handle the future, and make the most of the time He has given you today. And remember, nothing is too difficult for God, and no dreams are too big for Him—not even yours.

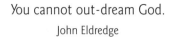

You cannot out-dream God.
John Eldredge

Allow your dreams a place in your prayers and plans.
God-given dreams can help you move into
the future He is preparing for you.
Barbara Johnson

The future lies all before us. Shall it only be a slight advance
upon what we usually do? Ought it not to be a bound,
a leap forward to altitudes of endeavor
and success undreamed of before?
Annie Armstrong

Set goals so big that unless God helps you,
you will be a miserable failure.
Bill Bright

Making your dreams come true requires work. John Maxwell writes, "The gap between your vision and your present reality can only be filled through a commitment to maximize your potential." Enough said.

Who Are You?
You Are a Person Who Puts
Faith Above Feelings

Now the just shall live by faith.
Hebrews 10:38 NKJV

Hebrews 10:38 teaches that we should live by faith. Yet sometimes, despite our best intentions, negative feelings can rob us of the peace and abundance that would otherwise be ours through Christ. When anger or anxiety separates us from the spiritual blessings that God has in store, we must rethink our priorities and renew our faith. And we must place faith above feelings. Human emotions are highly variable, decidedly unpredictable, and often unreliable. Our emotions are like the weather, only far more fickle. So we must learn to live by faith, not by the ups and downs of our own emotional roller coasters.

Sometime during this day, you will probably be gripped by a strong negative emotion. Distrust it. Reign it in. Test it. And turn it over to God. Your emotions will inevitably change; God will not. So trust Him completely as you watch your feelings slowly evaporate into thin air—which, of course, they will.

I do not need to feel good or be ecstatic in order
to be in the center of God's will.

Bill Bright

We are to live by faith, not feelings.

Kay Arthur

Instead of waiting for the feeling, wait upon God.
You can do this by growing still and quiet, then expressing in
prayer what your mind knows is true about Him,
even if your heart doesn't feel it at this moment.

Shirley Dobson

Discipleship is a decision to live by what I know
about God, not by what I feel about him
or myself or my neighbors.

Eugene Peterson

Here are the facts: God's love is real; His peace is real; His
support is real. Don't ever let your emotions obscure these
facts.

Who Are You?
You Are a Person Who
Doesn't Act Impulsively

*Even zeal is not good without knowledge,
and the one who acts hastily sins.*
Proverbs 19:2 HCSB

M aybe you've heard this old saying: "Look before you leap." Well, that saying may be old, but it still applies to you. Before you jump into something, you should look ahead and plan ahead. Otherwise, you might soon be sorry you jumped!

When you acquire the habit of planning ahead, you'll usually make better choices. So when it comes to the important things in life, make a plan and stick to it. When you do, you'll think about the consequences of your actions before you do something silly . . . or dangerous . . . or both.

Allow your dreams a place in your prayers and plans.
God-given dreams can help you move into the future
He is preparing for you.

Barbara Johnson

Faith in God will not get for you everything you want,
but it will get for you what God wants you to have.
The unbeliever does not need what he wants;
the Christian should want only what he needs.

Vance Havner

The only way you can experience abundant life is
to surrender your plans to Him.

Charles Stanley

Wisdom always waits for the right time to act,
while emotion always pushes for action right now.

Joyce Meyer

The best time to decide how you're going to behave is before
you find yourself in a difficult (or tempting) situation. So think
ahead, plan ahead, and follow your plan!

Who Are You?
You Are a Person Who Understands the Need to Make Good Decisions

If you need wisdom—if you want to know what God wants you to do—ask him, and he will gladly tell you. He will not resent your asking.

James 1:5 NLT

L ife presents each of us with countless questions, conundrums, doubts, and problems. Thankfully, the riddles of everyday living are not too difficult to solve if we look for answers in the right places. When we have questions, we should consult God's Word, we should consult our own consciences, and we should consult a few close friends and family members.

Perhaps Søren Kierkegaard was stating the obvious when he observed, "Life can only be understood backwards; but it must be lived forwards." Still, Kierkegaard's words are far easier to understand than they are to live by.

Taking a forward-looking (and stress-conquering) approach to life means learning the art of solving difficult problems sensibly and consistently . . . and sooner rather than later.

No trumpets sound when the important decisions
of our life are made. Destiny is made known silently.
Agnes DeMille

Life is built on character, but character is built on decisions.
Warren Wiersbe

The Reference Point for the Christian is the Bible.
All values, judgments, and attitudes must be gauged in
relationship to this Reference Point.
Ruth Bell Graham

Successful people make right decisions early
and manage those decisions daily.
John Maxwell

Never take on a major obligation of any kind without first
taking sufficient time to carefully consider whether or not
you should commit to it. The bigger the obligation, the more
days you should take to decide. If someone presses you for an
answer before you are ready, your automatic answer should
always be "No."

Who Are You?
You Are a Person Who Dates Wisely

Do not be mismatched with unbelievers. For what partnership is there between righteousness and lawlessness? Or what fellowship does light have with darkness?
2 Corinthians 6:14 HCSB

Is God a part of your dating life? Hopefully so. If you sincerely want to know God, they you should date people who feel the same way.

If you're still searching for Mr. or Mrs. Right (while trying to avoid falling in love with Mr. or Mrs. Wrong), be patient, be prudent, and be picky. Look for someone whose values you respect, whose behavior you approve of, and whose faith you admire. Remember that appearances can be deceiving and tempting, so watch your step. And when it comes to the important task of building a lifetime relationship with the guy or girl of your dreams, pray about it!

When it comes to your dating life, God wants to give His approval—or not—but He won't give it until He's asked. So ask, listen, and decide accordingly.

The beauty of any relationship that bears fruit and life is that it is entered into of and by one's own choice.

Dennis Jernigan

Line by line, moment by moment, special times are etched into our memories in the permanent ink of everlasting love in our relationships.

Gloria Gaither

It wasn't the apple, it was the pair.

Anonymous

The single most important element in any human relationship is honesty—with oneself, with God, and with others.

Catherine Marshall

Be choosy: Don't ever "settle" for second-class treatment—you deserve someone who values you as a person . . . and shows it.

Who Are You?
You Are a Person Who Understands That Every Day Is a New Beginning

You are being renewed in the spirit of your minds;
you put on the new man, the one created according to
God's likeness in righteousness and purity of the truth.
Ephesians 4:23-24 HCSB

Each new day offers countless opportunities to serve God, to seek His will, and to obey His teachings. But each day also offers countless opportunities to stray from God's commandments and to wander far from His path.

Sometimes, we wander aimlessly in a wilderness of our own making, but God has better plans for us. And, whenever we ask Him to renew our strength and guide our steps, He does so.

Consider this day a new beginning. Consider it a fresh start, a renewed opportunity to serve your Creator with willing hands and a loving heart. Ask God to renew your sense of purpose as He guides your steps. Today is a glorious opportunity to serve God. Seize that opportunity while you can; tomorrow may indeed be too late.

No matter how badly we have failed,
we can always get up and begin again.
Our God is the God of new beginnings.

Warren Wiersbe

Sometimes your medicine bottle has on it,
"Shake well before using." That is what God has to do
with some of His people. He has to shake them well
before they are ever usable.

Vance Havner

No man need stay the way he is.

Harry Emerson Fosdick

More often than not, when something looks like
it's the absolute end, it is really the beginning.

Charles Swindoll

God wants to give you peace, and He wants to renew your spirit. It's up to you to slow down and give Him a chance to do so.

Who Are You?
You Are a Person Who Understands
That God Doesn't Change

For I am the Lord, I do not change.
Malachi 3:6 NKJV

We live in a world that is always changing, but we worship a God that never changes—thank goodness! That means that we can be comforted in the knowledge that our Heavenly Father is the rock that simply cannot be moved: "I am the Lord, I do not change" (Malachi 3:6 NKJV).

The next time you face difficult circumstances, tough times, unfair treatment, or unwelcome changes, remember that some things never change—things like the love that you feel in your heart for your family and friends . . . and the love that God feels for you. So, instead of worrying too much about life's inevitable challenges, focus your energies on finding solutions. Have faith in your own abilities, do your best to solve your problems, and leave the rest up to God.

The secret of contentment in the midst of change is
found in having roots in the changeless Christ—
the same yesterday, today and forever.

Ed Young

The resurrection of Jesus Christ is the power of God to
change history and to change lives.

Bill Bright

Conditions are always changing; therefore,
I must not be dependent upon conditions. What matters
supremely is my soul and my relationship to God.

Corrie ten Boom

With God, it isn't who you were that matters;
it's who you are becoming.

Liz Curtis Higgs

The world continues to change, as do you. Change is
inevitable—you can either roll with it or be rolled over by it.
In order to avoid the latter, you should choose the former . . .
and trust God as you go.

Who Are You?
You Are a Person Who Meets
with God Every Morning

Morning by morning he wakens me and opens my understanding to his will. The Sovereign Lord has spoken to me, and I have listened.

Isaiah 50:4-5 NLT

Want to know God better? Then schedule a meeting with Him every day.

Daily life is a tapestry of habits, and no habit is more important to your spiritual health than the discipline of daily prayer and devotion to the Creator. When you begin each day with your head bowed and your heart lifted, you are reminded of God's love and God's laws.

When you do engage in a regular regimen of worship and praise, God will reward you for your wisdom and your obedience. Each new day is a gift from God, and if you're wise, you'll spend a few quiet moments thanking the Giver. It's a wonderful way to start your day.

The moment you wake up each morning, all your wishes
and hopes for the day rush at you like wild animals.
And the first job each morning consists in shoving it all back;
in listening to that other voice, taking that other point of
view, letting that other, larger, stronger,
quieter life coming flowing in.

C. S. Lewis

A person with no devotional life generally struggles
with faith and obedience.

Charles Stanley

Mark it down. God never turns away the honest seeker.
Go to God with your questions. You may not find all the
answers, but in finding God, you know the One who does.

Max Lucado

Maintenance of the devotional mood is indispensable
to success in the Christian life.

A. W. Tozer

You need to talk to your Creator every day. God is ready to
talk to you, and you should be ready to talk to Him first thing
every morning.

Who Are You?
You Are a Person Who Uses Your Gifts

I remind you to keep ablaze the gift of God that is in you.
2 Timothy 1:6 HCSB

How do we thank God for the gifts He has given us? By using those gifts, that's how!

God has given you talents and opportunities that are uniquely yours. Are you willing to use your gifts in the way that God intends? And are you willing to summon the discipline that is required to develop your talents and to hone your skills? That's precisely what God wants you to do, and that's precisely what you should desire for yourself.

As you seek to expand your talents, you will undoubtedly encounter stumbling blocks along the way, such as the fear of rejection or the fear of failure. When you do, don't stumble! Just continue to refine your skills, and offer your services to God. And when the time is right, He will use you—but it's up to you to be thoroughly prepared when He does.

You are the only person on earth
who can use your ability.
Zig Ziglar

God often reveals His direction for our lives through
the way He made us . . .
with a certain personality and unique skills.
Bill Hybels

The Lord has abundantly blessed me all of my life.
I'm not trying to pay Him back for all of His wonderful gifts;
I just realize that He gave them to me to give away.
Lisa Whelchel

God has given you special talents—
now it's your turn to give them back to God.
Marie T. Freeman

God has given you a unique array of talents and opportunities. If you use your gifts wisely, they're multiplied. If you misuse your gifts—or ignore them altogether—they are lost. God is anxious for you to use your gifts . . . are you?

Who Are You?
You Are a Person Who Trusts God's Plans

*You reveal the path of life to me; in Your presence is
abundant joy; in Your right hand are eternal pleasures.*
Psalm 16:11 HCSB

The Bible makes it clear: God's got a plan—a very big plan—and you're an important part of that plan. But here's the catch: God won't force His plans upon you; you've got to figure things out for yourself . . . or not.

As a follower of Christ, you should ask yourself this question: "How closely can I make my plans match God's plans?" The more closely you manage to follow the path that God intends for your life, the better.

Do you have questions or concerns about your relationships? Take them to God in prayer. Do you have hopes and expectations? Talk to God about your dreams. Are you carefully planning for the days and weeks ahead? Consult God as you establish your priorities. Turn every concern over to your Heavenly Father, and sincerely seek His guidance—prayerfully, earnestly, and often. Then, listen for His answers . . . and trust the answers that He gives.

God possesses infinite knowledge and awareness
which is uniquely His. At all times, even in the midst
of any type of suffering, I can realize that he knows,
loves, watches, understands, and more than that,
He has a purpose.

Billy Graham

I don't doubt that the Holy Spirit guides your decisions
from within when you make them with the intention
of pleasing God. The error would be to think that
He speaks only within, whereas in reality He speaks
also through Scripture, the Church,
Christian friends, and books.

C. S. Lewis

The God who orchestrates the universe has
a good many things to consider that have not occurred
to me, and it is well that I leave them to Him.

Elisabeth Elliot

When life seems unfair, try spending more time trusting God
and less time dwelling on "the unfairness of it all."

Who Are You?
You Are a Person Who Puts Holiness Before Happiness

Blessed are those who hunger and thirst for righteousness, because they will be filled.
Matthew 5:6 HCSB

Because you are an imperfect human being, you are not "perfectly" happy—and that's perfectly okay with God. He is far less concerned with your happiness than He is with your holiness.

God continuously reveals Himself in everyday life, but He does not do so in order to make you contented; He does so in order to lead you to His Son. So don't be overly concerned with your current level of happiness; it will change. Be more concerned with the current state of your relationship with Christ: He does not change. And because your Savior transcends time and space, you can be comforted in the knowledge that in the end, His joy will become your joy . . . for all eternity.

You don't have to be like the world to have an impact on the world. You don't have to be like the crowd to change the crowd. You don't have to lower yourself down to their level to lift them up to your level.
Holiness doesn't seek to be odd.
Holiness seeks to be like God.

Max Lucado

Holiness isn't in a style of dress. It's not a matter of rules and regulations. It's a way of life that emanates quietness and rest, joy in family, shared pleasures with friends, the help of a neighbor—and the hope of a Savior.

Joni Eareckson Tada

Our ultimate aim in life is not to be healthy, wealthy, prosperous, or problem free.
Our ultimate aim in life is to bring glory to God.

Anne Graham Lotz

God is holy and wants you to be holy. Christ died to make you holy. Make sure that your response to Christ's sacrifice is worthy of Him.

Who Are You?
You Are a Person Who Entrusts the Future to God

*"I say this because I know what I am planning for you,"
says the Lord. "I have good plans for you, not plans to hurt you.
I will give you hope and a good future."*

Jeremiah 29:11 NCV

How can you make smart choices if you're unwilling to trust God and obey Him? The answer, of course, is that you can't. That's why you should trust God in everything (and that means entrusting your future to God).

How bright is your future? Well, if you're a faithful believer, God's plans for you are so bright that you'd better wear shades. But here are some important follow-up questions: How bright do you believe your future to be? Are you expecting a terrific tomorrow, or are you dreading a terrible one? The answers you give will have a powerful impact on the way tomorrow turns out.

Do you trust in the ultimate goodness of God's plan for your life? Will you face tomorrow's challenges with optimism and hope? You should. After all, God created you for a very important reason: His reason. And you have important work to do: His work.

Today, as you live in the present and look to the future, remember that God has an amazing plan for you. Act—and believe—accordingly.

We must trust as if it all depended on God
and work as if it all depended on us.
C. H.. Spurgeon

Every man lives by faith, the nonbeliever
as well as the saint; the one by faith in natural laws
and the other by faith in God.
A. W. Tozer

Faith in faith is pointless.
Faith in a living, active God moves mountains.
Beth Moore

Hope for the future isn't some pie-in-the-sky dream; hope for the future is simply one aspect of trusting God.

Who Are You?
You Are a Person Who Avoids People Who Behave Foolishly

Do not be deceived: "Bad company corrupts good morals."
I Corinthians 15:33 HCSB

If you hang out with people who do dumb things, pretty soon, you'll probably find yourself doing dumb things, too. And that's bad . . . very bad. So here's an ironclad rule for earning more self-respect and more rewards from life: If your peer group is headed in the wrong direction, find another peer group, and fast. Otherwise, before you know it, you'll be caught up in trouble that you didn't create and you don't deserve.

When you feel pressured to do things—or to say things—that lead you away from God, you're heading straight for trouble. So don't do the "easy" thing or the "popular" thing. Do the right thing, and don't worry about winning any popularity contests.

Tell me what company you keep,
and I'll tell you what you are.

Miguel de Cervantes

Those who follow the crowd usually get lost in it.

Rick Warren

We, as God's people, are not only to stay far away
from sin and sinners who would entice us,
but we are to be so like our God that we mourn over sin.

Kay Arthur

A person who deliberately and habitually sins is
proving that he does not know Christ
and therefore cannot be abiding in Him.

Warren Wiersbe

A thoughtful Christian doesn't follow the crowd . . . a thoughtful Christian follows Jesus (and he feels better about himself when he does).

Who Are You?
You Are a Person Who Forgives People Sooner Rather Than Later

You have heard that it was said, You shall love your neighbor and hate your enemy. But I tell you, love your enemies, and pray for those who persecute you.
Matthew 5:43-44 HCSB

It's hard to feel good about yourself while you're carrying around a heart full of bitterness. That's one reason (but not the only reason) that you should be quick to forgive everybody.

If there exists even one person whom you have not forgiven (and that includes yourself), follow God's commandment and His will for your life: forgive that person today. And remember that bitterness, anger, and regret are not part of God's plan for your life. Forgiveness is.

If you sincerely wish to forgive someone, pray for that person. And then pray for yourself by asking God to heal your heart. Don't expect forgiveness to be easy or quick, but rest assured: with God as your partner, you can forgive . . . and you will.

God expects us to forgive others as He has forgiven us;
we are to follow His example by having a forgiving heart.

Vonette Bright

To be a Christian means to forgive the inexcusable,
because God has forgiven the inexcusable in you.

C. S. Lewis

Our Lord worked with people as they were,
and He was patient—not tolerant of sin,
but compassionate.

Vance Havner

Forgiveness is the key that unlocks the door of resentment
and the handcuffs of hate. It is a power that breaks
the chains of bitterness and the shackles of selfishness.

Corrie ten Boom

When other people have made a mistake . . . it's a mistake not
to forgive them.

Who Are You?
You Are a Person Who Strives to Be a Good Example

For am I now trying to win the favor of people, or God?
Or am I striving to please people?
If I were still trying to please people,
I would not be a slave of Christ.
Galatians 1:10 HCSB

Whether you like it or not, you simply can't deny the fact that you're an example to other people. The question is not whether you will be an example to your family and friends; the question is precisely what kind of example will you be.

Corrie ten Boom advised, "Don't worry about what you do not understand. Worry about what you do understand in the Bible but do not live by." And that's sound advice because your family, friends, and dates are always watching . . . and so, for that matter, is God.

Too many Christians have geared their program to please,
to entertain, and to gain favor from this world.
We are concerned with how much, instead of how little,
like this age we can become.

Billy Graham

Nothing speaks louder or more powerfully
than a life of integrity.

Charles Swindoll

In your desire to share the gospel,
you may be the only Jesus someone else will ever meet.
Be real and be involved with people.

Barbara Johnson

The sermons you live drown out the ones you give.

Criswell Freeman

If you're a Christian, behave like one. The sermons you live are
far more important than the sermons you preach.

Who Are You?
You Are a Person Who Has
a Healthy Fear of God

Since we are receiving a Kingdom that cannot be destroyed,
let us be thankful and please God by worshiping
him with holy fear and awe.

Hebrews 12:28 NLT

D o you possess a healthy, fearful respect for God's pow-er? Hopefully so. After all, the lesson from the book of Proverbs is clear: "The fear of the Lord is the begin-ning of knowledge, but fools despise wisdom and instruction" (1:7 NKJV). Yet, you live in a world that often ignores the role that God plays in shaping the affairs of mankind. You live in a world where too many people consider it "unfashionable" or "unseemly" to discuss the fear of God. Don't count yourself among their number.

God maintains absolute sovereignty over His creation, and His power is beyond comprehension. As believers, we must cultivate a sincere respect for God's awesome power. The fear of the Lord is, indeed, the beginning of knowledge. So today, as you face the realities of everyday life, remember this: until you acquire a healthy, respectful fear of God's power, your education is incomplete, and so is your faith.

When true believers are awed by the greatness of God
and by the privilege of becoming His children,
then they become sincerely motivated, effective evangelists.

Bill Hybels

A healthy fear of God will do much to deter us from sin.

Charles Swindoll

The fear of God is the death of every other fear.

C. H. Spurgeon

The remarkable thing about fearing God is that
when you fear God, you fear nothing else,
whereas if you do not fear God, you fear everything else.

Oswald Chambers

It's the right kind of fear: Your respect for God should make you
fearful of disobeying Him . . . very fearful.

Who Are You?
You Are a Person Who Accepts God's Priceless Gift

Don't love the world's ways. Don't love the world's goods. Love of the world squeezes out love for the Father. Practically everything that goes on in the world—wanting your own way, wanting everything for yourself, wanting to appear important— has nothing to do with the Father. It just isolates you from him. The world and all its wanting, wanting, wanting is on the way out—but whoever does what God wants is set for eternity.

1 John 2:15-17 MSG

Eternal life is not an event that begins when you die. Eternal life begins when you invite Jesus into your heart right here on earth. So it's important to remember that God's plans for you are not limited to the ups and downs of everyday life. If you've allowed Jesus to reign over your heart, you've already begun your eternal journey.

As mere mortals, our vision for the future, like our lives here on earth, is limited. God's vision is not burdened by such limitations: His plans extend throughout all eternity.

Let us praise the Creator for His priceless gift, and let us share the Good News with all who cross our paths. We return our Father's love by accepting His grace and by sharing His message and His love. When we do, we are blessed here on earth and throughout all eternity.

Teach us to set our hopes on heaven, to hold firmly to the promise of eternal life, so that we can withstand the struggles and storms of this world.

Max Lucado

Your choice to either receive or reject the Lord Jesus Christ will determine where you spend eternity.

Anne Graham Lotz

And because we know Christ is alive, we have hope for the present and hope for life beyond the grave.

Billy Graham

I know, Lord, that this world is not my home; I am only here for a brief while. And, You have given me the priceless gift of eternal life through Your Son Jesus. Keep the hope of heaven fresh in my heart, and, while I am in this world, help me to pass through it with faith in my heart and praise on my lips . . . for You. Amen